The Early Poetry of
William Carlos Williams

ALSO BY ROD TOWNLEY

Blue Angels Black Angels

The Early Poetry of
William Carlos Williams

ROD TOWNLEY

Cornell University Press | ITHACA AND LONDON

This book is for
Dwight Macdonald

Preface

Most of the poems discussed in this work can be found in two books by Williams: *The Collected Earlier Poems* and *Imaginations*, both published by New Directions Publishing Corporation, New York. Since not every reader will have these books readily at hand, I have quoted a number of poems in their entirety.

In addition, where it has seemed appropriate, I have made available previously unpublished primary sources, not merely as supports to my argument, but as artifacts in themselves, independent of the critical uses to which I put them. Two appendices house most of these artifacts. Appendix A contains a suite of poems from about 1915, previously unavailable in print, collectively titled (by Williams) "Pastorals and Self-Portraits." Appendix B contains selections from a medical file that Williams kept active between 1908 and 1911.

I would like to thank the following people for their encouragement and assistance: Else Albrecht-Carrié, Walter Bezanson, Libby Blackman, Robert Bly, Paul Fussell, Donald Gallup, Karl Gay, Edith Heal, James Laughlin, David Leverenz, Cosima Long, Robert Mulligan, Joel Oppenheimer, Emily Mitchell Wallace, Neda M. Westlake, Anne Whelpley, Dr. William Eric Williams.

ROD TOWNLEY

Philadelphia, Pennsylvania

Contents

Abbreviations

Works

Auto.   *The Autobiography of William Carlos Williams.* New York: Random House, 1952.

CEP   *The Collected Earlier Poems of William Carlos Williams.* Norfolk, Conn.: New Directions, 1951.

CLP   *The Collected Later Poems of William Carlos Williams.* Norfolk, Conn.: New Directions, 1950.

FD   *The Farmers' Daughters.* Norfolk, Conn.: New Directions, 1961.

IAG   *In the American Grain.* New York: Albert and Charles Boni, 1925.

Imag.   *Imaginations,* ed. Webster Schott. New York: New Directions, 1970. (Reprints five early works: *Kora in Hell: Improvisations, Spring and All, The Great American Novel, A Novelette and Other Prose,* and "The Descent of Winter.")

IWWP   *I Wanted to Write a Poem: The Autobiography of the Works of a Poet,* ed. Edith Heal. Boston: Beacon Press, 1958.

Pat.   *Paterson.* New York: New Directions, 1963.

PFB   *Pictures from Brueghel,* New York: New Directions, 1965. (Also contains *The Desert Music* and *Journey to Love.*)

SE   *Selected Essays of William Carlos Williams.* New York: Random House, 1954; reprinted by New Directions, 1959.

SL   *Selected Letters of William Carlos Williams,* ed. John C. Thirlwall. New York: McDowell, Obolensky, 1957.

Manuscript Collections

L   The Lockwood Memorial Library, State University of
         New York at Buffalo.
VP   The Van Pelt Library, University of Pennsylvania.
YALC   Yale American Literature Collection, in the Beinecke Rare
         Book and Manuscript Library, Yale University.

The Early Poetry of
William Carlos Williams

Introduction

"The undersigned protest the pseudo-paternalistic attitudes of those who award prizes in poetic beauty contests," scribbled Robert Kelly on the bulletin board at the 1971 National Poetry Festival in Allendale, Michigan. "No more masterpieces!" he concluded, recalling Artaud's dictum. Among the signers was Diane Wakoski, who added in parentheses after her name, "Poets are not race-horses."

Of course, the contest was held anyway, a winner announced and roundly booed, but the feeling of the nine-day festival was clearly on the side of Kelly's conspirators rather than on that of the festival organizers. One feels Williams would have been pleased. He would have recognized that fierce underdog pride which pervaded even the most casual conversations and reminiscences. Prizes were given by "the other guys" to their own kind, to the spiritual children of Eliot, not to the children of Olson and Williams. Such an attitude, of course, ignores the various honors (including the Dial Award, the National Book Award, and the Pulitzer Prize) that Williams himself received.

Yet the Williams/Eliot feud, fifty years old now, has never been resolved, perhaps because the old confusions remain at the heart of it. A poet may decide to drop out of the race for prizes, yet he still hopes to produce poems that will live in mankind's memory. To produce such poems, he must be "better"—and recognized as better—than other poets. These others tend to become the "competition," sometimes even the "enemy."

Destructive competitiveness is an inherent danger, but not the exclusive fault, of the concept of the literary masterpiece. To do away with the concept would, for some poets, be to throw away the baby with the bath water. For other poets, equally talented but of a different temperament, the concept would not be missed, because it has never been invoked. In fact, several of the most important American poets (Williams among them) have not produced masterpieces in the old, grand sense. They are led by different incentives, by devious means, to indeterminate ends.

Reading through the collected poetry of Williams, one senses the futility of pointing to this or that poem as a masterpiece, or even as being much better than those that precede or follow it. Certainly there are great moments and there are lapses, but they seem to be functions of one another, different but connected parts of a living body of work. It is at first disconcerting to realize that one can read through the entire opus, some fifty volumes of prose and poetry (and what seems an almost equal amount of unpublished material), be enthralled by much of it, recognize its importance in the development of American literature, and at the end still have to ask oneself, "Is it any good?" Somehow it all goes too fast; one poem goes on to another without calling attention to itself or stopping the reader for anything more than a laugh of delight. Where are the masterpieces? To be sure, critical efforts have been made to single out certain poems; for example, "The Red Wheelbarrow," "Spring and All," and "The Yachts," the latter one of his least characteristic works. But it is useless. Williams simply did not have the progressive, summative turn of mind that permits some artists to move from pinnacle to pinnacle of achievement. The pinnacles are after all no more important than the valleys or the Hackensack meadows or the back yard. He could never sympathize with or even truly understand Pound's assumption that poems are made from other poems, that mind fertilizes mind, piling masterpiece on masterpiece like cities in the sky, or that the environment is (in Pound's words) "putty" to be used, ignored, or (if one's passport is in order) escaped. To Williams, the environment, like one's body, is part of one's identity. The deeper the roots, the stronger the sense of self. Williams' work must be understood "somatically," as the work of a man living by all six senses inside his own body to create a corresponding body of work. The poems do not "stop" the reader because they are finally inseparable, one from another, like the limbs of a man or of a tree.

Each poem is a fragment of the fluidic imaginative world in which we all live and dream, distinct from but coterminous with the actual world. The paradox must be seen clearly: the poems are inseparable, yet each is a shrapnel-like fragment. As Williams said of his work in an interview in the New York *Herald Tribune* (January 18, 1932), it is "in tune with the tempo of [my] life—scattered, yet welded into a whole; broken, yet woven together." In the welding and the weaving one discovers the techniques (often brilliant) of Williams' poetry.

Many good poets draw to some extent on unconscious resources, but at times in Williams' work there is a veritable surrender to the psychic tide, followed immediately by an assertion of conscious control to prevent drowning. "The

Sea-Elephant" is Williams' self-portrait, the breathing mam-mal who lives in water:

> Swing—ride
> walk
> on wires—toss balls
> stoop and
>
> contort yourselves—
> But I
> am love. I am
> from the sea—
>
> Blouaugh!   [*CEP*, 73]

Although Williams was concerned with form, there are few major poets who interfere so little with the instinctive poetic gesture. Eliot searches mythology for archetypal images, then shapes them by the power of his intense conscious mind into extraordinary poems. He is slumming in the unconscious.

The unconscious is not always a clean or well-lighted place. Williams' early poem "The Wanderer" ends with the poet's baptism in "the Passaic, that filthy river," a scene which most critics see as evidence that the young poet was at last renounc-ing the romantic diction and mythological ladies of his first poems and turning to the local environment for his inspiration and patterns of speech. This is part of it; but one mustn't for-get that the subject is baptism—and death—and that "The Wanderer" is a religious poem.

> Then the river began to enter my heart,
>
> . . . . .
>
> Till I felt the utter depth of its rottenness
> The vile breadth of its degradation
> And dropped down knowing this was me now.
>
> [*CEP*, 11]

The descent into the self, then deeper, into the "collective

unconscious" proposed by Jung, leads one through terror to
a kind of hopeless security. What one writes from such a position cannot be predicted, but it is unlikely to be a sonnet or
a villanelle. In Williams' case, the results are various, but most
often they embody the paradox mentioned above: the imagistic fragment and the dreamlike flow. Whatever passes before
the poet's eyes is his subject, and yet back of it all is the awareness of the river down which everything, including the poet
himself, is floating. Thus the "contradictions" in Williams'
statements about poetry: "Works of art . . . must be real,
not 'realism' but reality itself—" (*Imag.*, 117); "The poem is
a dream" (*SE*, 281).[1]

Such statements, and such poems as "The Wanderer," suggest numerous questions, some of which will be faced, if not
answered, in the chapters that follow. How, for example, did
Williams' emotional and spiritual crises (so far as they can be
analyzed) affect his approach to his work, the way he went
about getting it done? Where does the duality in his work,
the "fragment" and the "flow," originate, and what are its
consequences? Most important, how did his work change,
what were the real shifts, the real gains, as reflected in the
three or four major works composed before 1923?

These introductory pages are meant simply to indicate a
viable approach to Williams' work, and by extension to the
work of a large number of poets who learned from him.
Their position is summed up in the first sentence of the first
issue of *Contact* (December 1920), where Williams (or his
coeditor McAlmon) asserts "the conviction . . . that the
artist works to express perceptions rather than to attain standards of achievement." This does not mean that Williams
denies the existence or the importance of aesthetic standards,
provided they inhere in life and are not mere cultural over-

lays which time will efface. "For if there are standards in
reality and in existence," the editorial goes on, "if there are
values and relations which are absolute, they will apply to
art. Otherwise any standard of criticism is a mere mental exercise." These statements are difficult to understand in any
precise sense, and one feels that the two young editors were
themselves fishing for what they meant to say. It is the emphasis that matters: standards, yes, if they are "real"; discrim-
inations must be made. But art's special usefulness, not just
its beauty or aesthetic perfection, is what provides its final
justification. By expressing his perceptions, the artist completes the act of perceiving, completes the contact, so that
reality is allowed the relief of becoming real—for the first
time truly available. To this end the process of continued creation may be more important to some artists than the accumu-
lation of discrete artifacts. As Williams says of Shakespeare,
he makes one object then pushes on "to make another, and another—perfectly blank to him as soon as they are completed"
(*SE*, 56). For the poet, the fashioning of the artifact is an act
of self-obliteration and self-renewal, "in which he keeps alive
by losing his life," as Williams says in the same essay. "In the
destructive element immerse," Conrad had put it years before,
though it is unlikely that he had the Passaic River in mind.
But the diving, the dying into the poem for the world's sal-
vation, is the same. It is the new prayer and, like prayer, is
most useful as a habitual, if possible a daily, action. The efficacy of the poem, seen in this way, depends upon its precision, which is its chastity, and upon its faithfulness to the
terms that it sets up. If the poem is a "masterpiece," so much
the better. But what matters most is the next poem, and the
next, getting in again and staying close.

 For Williams, and for the many his example has helped or

hindered, there are two kinds of poets: the spenders and the savers, the generators and the curators, those who plunge and those who shore fragments against their ruins. The scheme is too simple, of course. There are not two, or twenty-two, kinds of poets. But the aesthetic Manichaeism proceeds from fundamental divisions in Williams' psyche—perhaps in the American psyche; and anyone attempting an assessment of Williams would do well to approach his work from the same general direction from which Williams himself approached it.

His best poems are all rooted in the American frontier, the real one: the exact place (on the page) where the mind and the continent meet, edge to edge. In that wild locale, where the world roars before one's eyes like a waterfall or a locomotive, words like "masterpiece" are not wrong or offensive. They are simply inaudible.

CHAPTER ONE

Early Years, 1900–1909

An old rabbi was once asked why no one nowadays sees God. The sage replied that people are not willing to look that low. In his early apprenticeship to poetry, Williams was unwilling to look that low. In 1920, near the end of that apprenticeship, he could write to his friend Alva N. Turner, "You count yourself one of the most unhappy of mortals and you are so. . . . It is so because you are wise, because you are not satisfied to look only up but also down" (*SL*, 46). In 1903, from his little room overlooking the pseudo-medieval quadrangle and turreted gatehouse of the University of Pennsylvania, Williams contemplated the lofty beauties of Romantic and Victorian poetry while striving in his studies and other activities to live up to the Puritan ideals of conscientiousness, hard work, and moral rectitude. "I'm afraid I *was* a rather sanctimonious young man," he admitted later (*IWWP*, 3).

He was also an unhappy young man much of the time, subject to fits of moodiness and frequent (one suspects psychosomatic) sore throats. He wrote letter after letter to his mother minimizing as best he could his homesickness, and working himself up to a sort of daunted cheerfulness.[1] His main correspondents during his years in the Medical School at Penn were his mother (Raquel Hélène Williams) and his brother Edgar, one year his junior. With both he is always honest, earnest, and loving, but the details he chooses to write about differ interestingly according to which of them he is addressing. In 1904 he tells his mother of hearing each evening the vesper bells from the local nunnery; and the following year he tells her that he's off to church, where he hopes to get enough "calm inspiration" to last him for another seven days of hard studying. That same day he writes to Edgar enclosing a poem, now lost, called "Ode to My Appetite." There is no mention of church, just as there was no mention of a poem in the letter to his mother. In still another letter (November 12, 1905), he gives his brother an excited description of a football game, noting that everyone was going out afterwards to get drunk, a victory celebration. He concludes a bit mournfully that he wishes his conscience would let him join them in their revelry.

But his conscience did not let him; nor did it allow him to express, in those of his early poems that survive, anything much beyond awkward sublimity or awkward facetiousness (the latter the probable tone of "Ode to My Appetite"). Yet subversive tendencies are already apparent. With Edgar he can be himself, inhibited though that self still is; with his mother he is always his "better" self. The better self does not flirt with temptation and is unlikely to indulge in irreverent poems. "I have done things against my own feelings and convictions because you wanted me to," he writes to his mother, November 8, 1904. "Still, Mama dear, I know you are right and I am wrong" (SL, 7). It is a recurrent sentiment in the early correspondence.

Williams' better self wrote the poems he had Reid Howell print up for him in 1909. They look too high to see God, but his family approved of them. They are obedient poems. The Yale Library has a copy of the book (called simply *Poems*) covered with pencil markings by William G. Williams, his father, suggesting corrections for the second edition. Besides correcting spelling errors, Williams' father added a number of exclamation points and capital letters to make the sublime even sublimer. His son incorporated most of these changes in the new edition.

But no servility, no conscious subverting of his own ideals, colored this obedience. No doubt Williams felt, as strongly as in his *Autobiography* he says he felt in those early years, that "no one was ever going to be in a position to tell me what to write, and you can say that again. No one, and I meant no one (for money) was ever (never) going to tell me how or what I was going to write. That was number one" (*Auto.*, 49).

The foregoing statement is so emphatic as to be almost ambiguous, as if Williams' subconscious were working parenthetical sabotage. Yet in his conscious mind at least, Williams could not have been more fiercely independent. How is it, then, that those early poems are so derivative? Part of the answer is that Williams' ideas about poetry, quite confused at the time, were leading him in opposite directions, and he made a choice. Raised on Palgrave's *Golden Treasury*, Milton, and Keats—all that cozy sonority—he had also stumbled upon Walt Whitman's poetry—jagged and spontaneous, angles rather than curves—and he didn't know how to bring the two modes together. So he kept them apart. "My quick spontaneous poems, as opposed to my studied Keatsian sonnets, were written down in thick, stiff-covered copybooks. I can see them still, bound in marbelized paper. There were eighteen of them, full. . . . The copybook poems, my secret life, the poems I was writing before I met Pound, were what I can only describe as free verse, after Whitman" (*IWWP*, 5 and 8).[2]

This secret life he shared with no one. The poems he showed to Arlo Bates, his brother's English professor at M.I.T., were his sonnets and his long *Endymion* imitation. He timidly showed his friend Hilda Doolittle a sonnet, a serious meditation upon skunk cabbage. (It sent her into near hysterics.) As far as can be determined, he always chose his Keatsian poems to send to Edgar in the mail, along with some needed explanation as to what they meant. In a letter of January 17, 1906, for example, he unravels the allegorical meanings of an enclosed sonnet; he concludes by saying that people like to work for things before obtaining them and that a "judicious involvement of the meaning" is therefore wise. Even his prose style changes when he is talking about his sonnets. The "highbrow" words and stilted constructions warn the reader that the author is not just "Billy" Williams, but a young man whose artistic pretensions are equal to his great insecurity. Although he hated pose and sham, and criticized his schoolmate Ezra Pound for acting like a young Ronsard, Williams is himself posing in those of his early letters which deal with aesthetics. The poems he sent along with these letters are elaborately artificial, but at the same time intensely serious. He simply could not fight, except covertly in his secret notebooks, the great English literary tradition that he so much loved. Like Arjuna in *The Bhagavad-Gita* surveying the field before the battle, Williams looked over at the enemy and saw his teachers and well-wishers and loved ones. And so he continued with his involuted sonnets and allegories. "It was no language I spoke or even thought," he confessed later in life. "But it was my idea of what a poem should be" (*IWWP*,

14). It was most other people's idea of what poetry should be, too; and so he chose these poems to show them and to have a friend of his father's print up for him in 1909, while the eighteen notebooks of free verse sat on the shelf over his bed.

Since the "secret" notebooks have long since disappeared, one can only conjecture how imitation Whitman might compare with imitation Keats. It is tempting to assume that the Whitmanian mode was more suited to Williams' spontaneous temperament than the carefully symmetrical, smooth-honed manner of Keats; yet one must remember that Williams was a scientist and a persistently patient one at that. As Pound later wrote to him about their student days at Penn: "My early rekolektn is you in a room on the South side of the triange, and me sayin come on nowt, and you deciding on gawd an righteousness and the purrsuit of labour in the form of Dr. Gumbo's treatise on the lesions of the bungbone, or some other therapeutic compilation."[3] Still, the spontaneous, come-on-out aspect of his character cannot be denied. A poem he wrote when he was eighteen (which he claims to be the first poem he ever wrote) bears witness to this fresh, expulsive spirit, for it "was born like a bolt out of the blue. It came unsolicited and broke a spell of disillusion and suicidal despondency" (*Auto.*, 47). It reads:

> A black, black cloud
> flew over the sun
> driven by fierce flying
> rain.   [*IWWP*, 4; *Auto.*, 47]

K. L. Goodwin makes the intriguing observation that this little poem "does not differ in style from a great many poems written much later by Williams, poems like 'The Term' or the opening of 'To a Poor Old Woman.' Secondly, it is very like many 'imagist' poems, though Imagism as a movement was not inaugurated until 1908."[4] Drawing conclusions from a four-line scrap of verse is admittedly hazardous; but if Williams was in fact writing two different kinds of poetry right from the start—one exemplifying his "idea of what a poem should be," and the other his intuitive knowledge of what, for him, a poem was—some common critical notions about the development of Williams' style need to be reexamined.

An indispensable document in any such revaluation is a yellowed scrap of notebook paper discovered by Emily Mitchell Wallace in the archives of the Beinecke Library. It is a grade school composition with the author's full name "William Carlos Williams" carefully printed at the top.[5] On penciled lines drawn with the aid of a ruler, the ten- or eleven-year-old Williams had written a paragraph about a tree. This particular tree—perhaps one which the boy had observed in the neighborhood—bore a dying branch which drooped low over the sidewalk. The piece provides early evidence of Williams' life-long obsession with trees, particularly with flowering trees. But what is extraordinary is the use Williams made of it more than thirty years afterward. In 1926, making only the most minor changes, he typed the paragraph out into lines of poetry and sent it off to *The Dial*, where it was published in January 1927 under the title "Tree":

> The tree is stiff, the branch
> is arching, arching, arching
> to the ground. Already its tip
> reaches the hats of the passersby
> children leap at it, hang on it—
> bite on it. It is rotten, it
> will be thick with blossoms in
> the spring. Then it will break off

> of its own weight or from the pulls
> of the blossom seekers who will
> ravish it. Freed of this disgrace
> the tree will remain, stiffly upright

Emily Wallace's discussion of the poem is so sane, sensitive, and thorough that there is not much need to comment further.[6] Certainly it is not a major work, yet in its precocious sensuality ("bite on it," "ravish it") and in its spikey but coherent sound pattern there is a genuine infectiousness much like that which pervades his 1926 poem, "Young Sycamore" ("I must tell you"), or the 1915 poem, "Smell":

> and now it is the souring flowers of the bedraggled
> poplars: a festering pulp on the wet earth
> beneath them.   [*CEP*, 153]

It is not always easy to tell when Williams is being ingenuous and when he is being devious. Certainly, by sending "Tree" to *The Dial*, he was thumbing his nose at the critics, daring them to make what they would of his "new" poem. But he must also have recognized the poetic elements in his fifth-grade composition. He was always aware of the subtle relationship between poetry and common speech: "Under that language to which we have been listening all our lives a new, a more profound language, underlying all the dialectics offers itself. It is what they call poetry" (*Auto.*, 361). Without realizing what he was about, the young boy had been writing a kind of poetry, "hidden under the verbiage, seeking to be realized" (*Auto.*, 362). The fact that Williams could later speak of a poem as a "machine made of words" means only that he harbored and occasionally succeeded in uniting contrary theories of poetry. Poetry is something found. A poem is something made. His school piece was not a poem until he made it into one—but it was poetry from the start.

"Tree" is not the only poem to be rescued from oblivion. Writing to the editor of *Family Circle* (March 1972, p. 40) about the famous lyric "This Is Just To Say," Elizabeth Miller claims that "in a way it was I who saved that poem for posterity from the fate of the wastebasket. . . . Once [my husband and I] were visiting, and [Dr. Williams] was hunting through an assortment of papers for a poem he had just written for us to read. In this hunt a small sheet fell to the floor and I picked it up, read it and loved it immediately. 'Is this your poem of the day?' I asked. 'No,' he replied, 'that's just a note I wrote to Floss (his wife).' I insisted that although he might consider it just a note, I considered it a lovely *haiku*. . . . Needless to say, a lot of others think so, too." If the reader harbors the suspicion that something more than chance and less than Providence governed the fall of that particular scrap of paper, he is welcome to his speculations. Williams was capable of perfect ingenuousness and of extreme deviousness at every stage of his career, just as he was capable of opposite kinds of writing.

Perhaps feeling that he had perpetrated something of a hoax, Williams decided not to include "Tree" in his *Collected Earlier Poems*. But it deserves to be there. If the early, Whitmanesque notebooks contained many entries of this quality, their loss is grievous. Apparently, Williams was capable of writing excellently at ten and execrably at thirty, and vice versa. "Everything exists from the beginning" (*Imag.*, 158).

John C. Thirlwall's comments in "The Lost Poems of William Carlos Williams" (*New Directions 16*, 1957, 3–45) are typical of the sort of oversimplification to which Williams' early career has been subjected. Outlining a linear progress from "deplorable pastiches" (1906–1908) through "modified sonnets" (late 1909) to the publication of "Postlude" in *Des*

Imagistes (1913), Thirlwall concludes: "Since most of the practitioners of the New Poetry used Free Verse, Williams insensibly resorted to Free Verse, attracted by the Poundian-Imagist principle of direct treatment of the object, the rhythms of music rather than the beat of the metronome" (8). But as we have seen, Pound did not need to instruct Williams on the use of imagistic free verse, nor did Williams insensibly resort to it. The insensibility imputed to the poet is only in the mind of the critic.

One of the few critics to face Williams' aesthetic contradictions directly and to deal with them adequately is James E. Breslin.[7] Briefly, he argues that Williams' parents inhibited the boy's strong sensuality, thus creating the initial division within him. Both father and mother were "success-minded aliens in the New World," and both were, in different ways, "personally remote" (5). Breslin quotes descriptions in the *Autobiography* which suggest that Williams' mother was a medium whose frequent hallucinations and sudden, uncontrollable bouts of head-shaking terrified the young boy. Because of her, says Breslin, Williams became interested in painting; she led him to Palgrave's anthology, with its poems of dreamy optimism and dreamy pessimism; she led him to Keats. He thus became "a young man accustomed to thinking of the beautiful as the indistinct" (33). The frustration caused by his seeming acceptance of his mother's ideals is evident in the very existence of the subversive Whitman notebooks. These notebooks, suggests Breslin rather daringly, not having seen them, "provided expression for the buried life of the body that he always associated with Whitman" (7).

But literary as well as psychological reasons for Williams' conflicting poetic practices suggest themselves. During Williams' formative years, America was flooded with imitation

Victorian and pseudo-Georgian poetry. No one seemed to have any doubts about what poetry was or should be. It was apparently a genteel form of expression invented by the Romantics and brought to completion, purged of all grossness, by Tennyson. A fascinating book to consult in this connection is *The Younger American Poets*, by Jessie B. Rittenhouse (Boston, 1904). Its function was the same as that of numerous later volumes, such as Donald Allen's influential anthology, *The New American Poetry, 1945–1960:* to tell the news, to advertise, in the best sense, the work of poets who were still establishing their reputations. Among the fifteen poets included are Richard Hovey, a flamboyant imitator of Whitman's later style, whose *Songs From Vagabondia* young Williams and Pound both admired; Bliss Carman, whose sentences gallop on dactyls; Lizette Woodworth Reese, a precursor of H. D., who in a time of rococo diction concentrated on eliminating nonstructural ornament; Ridgely Torrence, Louise Imogen Guiney, and, surprisingly, George E. Santayana, at the time a prelapsarian sonneteer.

Rittenhouse makes some critical comments on Santayana which she almost surely would have repeated if she had seen Williams' early poetic efforts:

There is no evidence in Mr. Santayana's work that he is living in America in the twentieth century—and upon his own testimony he is not; he has withdrawn from the importunity of things:

> Within my nature's shell I slumber curled,
> Unmindful of the changing outer skies,—

and in this inviolate seclusion he enamels the pearl with the nacre of his own spirit. . . . His school is that of beauty; his time that of the gods; his faith the sanctity of loveliness; and his creed the restoration of the fair. [94–95]

Rittenhouse was one of the more exacting critics in a time
when, in Bogan's words, "the chief arbiters of the literary
world . . . were men whose timidity of spirit matched the
shallowness of their experience of life."[8] But even Rittenhouse, right on the mark though she is about Santayana's
verse, has a disconcerting habit of referring to poets as "sing-
ers," and praising them for their "heartening," "sympathetic,"
or "cheer-giving" songs. Without expatiating on the problems
inherent in impressionistic criticism, one may say of Rittenhouse, as to some extent of Williams himself, that her aesthetic
wobbles between a mushy, post-Victorian idealism on the one
hand, and a keen respect for verbal economy and world-
relatedness (it is too early to say "objective correlative") on
the other. Significantly, in writing about Lizette Woodworth
Reese, she manages within the same paragraph to liken her to
both Keats and Whitman—in fact quotes from the same Keats
poem from which Williams takes the epigraph to his own
first book. One might conclude that if Williams had come
across this study of the younger American poets of his day
he would not have been much helped by it, would in fact
have been confirmed in his own aesthetic contradictions.

At least Williams' contradictions had the advantage of being clear-cut. Those of Rittenhouse and many other critics of
the time were muddied by the fact that the Whitman they
saw and admired was the public bard. Williams was never
attracted by the "barbaric yawps" of the prophet. For him
Whitman's meaning was quite specific, even if still secret from
himself; it was "the buried life of the body," in Breslin's ex-
cellent phrase, as opposed to the rarified half-life of the spirit.
Immured within the Grecian urn was a living body, naked
and ignored. For Williams to be born again, the urn or protective shell would have to be shattered. "Before verse can be

human again it must learn to be brutal," wrote Synge in 1908.[9] No American critic could give advice of that kind, and years would pass before Williams could bring himself to follow it.

In 1908, Williams was concerned with the beautiful, not the brutal. As he wrote to Edgar six months before *Poems* came out, he was haunted by the idea that he could someday show the world "something more beautiful than it has ever seen before" (L). Earlier that year he had seen Isadora Duncan perform and wrote to Ed that he came away greatly excited by the "beauty of simple perfect truth." The beauty of truth? Truth of beauty? One can't get away from that "Ode on a Grecian Urn" for long in these early writings. From 1906 to 1909 Williams was interning at the French Hospital and the Nursery and Child's Hospital, both located on the West Side of Manhattan, working sometimes fourteen hours a day, performing appendectomies, delivering babies, and trying manfully to maintain his personal integrity while combating corruption among the hospital staff. To keep himself believing that truth and beauty were not mutually exclusive categories must have taken a colossal act of will.

In his last semester at Penn, he wrote an impassioned letter attempting to convince Edgar (and himself) that everything is good, and that one must love everything while striving to create immortal works of art. At several points in the letter, he emphasizes that these are not matters to be reasoned about. After a final admonishment to his brother, he closes, recommending Psalms 1, 23, and 37. Williams' fear of reasoning, and the strange fervor of his rhetoric, suggest psychological analogues to his religiosity. One is reminded of an unexplained statement on the first page of his *Autobiography:* "Terror dominated my youth, not fear . . . terror that flared from hidden places and all 'heaven.' " Terror of what? Williams does not pursue the subject, as if fifty years afterward it were still not to be reasoned about.

Whatever the cause of his terror, he seems to have reacted to it in two different ways. The first was to determine that he would be perfect: "Never to commit evil in any form, never especially to lie, to falsify, to deceive, but to tell the truth always, come what might of it" (*Auto.*, 27). The second was to try to show the world "something more beautiful than it has ever seen before." Truth and beauty, Whitman versus Keats, the acceptance of the world or its sublimation—the tension generated by these and other psychic opposites tore at Williams from within until he could not even reason about them safely.

"You see," he wrote to Marianne Moore a few years later, when he had achieved some objectivity on the matter, "I am a mixture of two bloods, neither of them particularly pure. Yet there is always in me a harking back to some sort of an aristocracy—probably of the gallows, or worse—that will have a hand in all my democratic impulses. Then again there is a certain broad-fingered strain in me that will always be handling an axe for budding King Charles Firsts. So I torture myself through life" (*SL*, 40). Almost nothing of the "broad-fingered strain" appears in the early Keatsian poems. Even the subject matter, except for a rare digression into "low" materials such as skunk cabbage, is unrelievedly aristocratic. In a 1906 letter to Edgar, Williams enclosed a long poem called "A Tragedy," involving an ill-fated love affair between a highborn lady and a neighboring swain. The twenty-three five-line stanzas of rhymed tetrameter are Coleridgean rather than Keatsian in tone, and suggest a recent reading of "Christabel." As in that poem, the action of "A Tragedy" takes place in the shadow of the mossy walls of an old mansion.

Christabel's father is no more dour and remote than the grey and grizzled father of Williams' heroine, nor is his language more painfully formal than that of the characters in Williams' poem. Implored by a lovesick swain to run away with him, the maiden replies that she will have to think about it for a day, weighing her love for him against her sense of duty to her father.

The real theme of the poem is not love but obedience. It is of course dangerous to try to extract biographical meanings from a poem whose incidents are entirely conventional and whose diction is derivative, but the heroine's dilemma does seem an externalization of Williams' own situation in 1906. Like the maiden, Williams loved his parents, but he felt distressed by their emotional remoteness, which was combined with a threatening brand of possessiveness. About halfway through the poem, the father catches the lovers together. Through an acceleration of the narrative movement at this point, Williams evokes the common adolescent terror of discovery in a sensual, therefore disloyal, situation. The consequences of the daughter's disobedience are tragic: a message miscarries, the lovers fail to meet at the appointed time, and the maid is left weeping in the archetypically furnished "trysting place": beneath a huge "knotted" tree beside a fountain and flowing brook. Then the last stanza:

> The night has reigned two lengthy hours.
> The birds have long since sought th[eir] nest[.]
> Upon the ground lies stretched the maid
> While kneeling o'er as though he prayed
> The father sooth[e]s her throbbing breast.   [VP]

Perhaps the aura of incest is unintentional, but the physical positions of the father and daughter, the ambiguity of "as though," and the adjective, "throbbing," invite the reader's speculations. Any biographical extrapolations to be made from this aspect of the poem, however, must be based upon the most tenuous of evidence. Better to ascribe the overtones to the influence of the Coleridge poem, with its aura of implicit sexual perversity.

"A Tragedy," ambitious as it is, represents little more than a warm-up for Williams' far more ambitious and in fact impossible project, the long *Endymion* imitation, which he slaved over for a number of years before throwing it into the furnace. Since Williams would doubtless have remembered the laborious transcription he had made of the poem for his friend Viola Baxter, his act of purgation by fire was not so radical or so courageous as the *Autobiography* would lead one to believe. He was not yet able to recognize "all that I must put from me / To come through ready for the high courses," as he puts the problem in his important poem of 1914, "The Wanderer" (*CEP*, 3).

He calls "The Wanderer" a reincarnation of his *Endymion* imitation, and in a sense it is. But the differences are profound. Since all that remains of the earlier poem is the long "Introduction" (YALC), it is difficult to know how much the wanderings of young Philip—the hero of that romantic saga—may have resembled the fantastic flights of his nameless modern counterpart in "The Wanderer." There is some similarity in the use of dream as a means of transportation, and a possible resemblance between the wandering poet's baptism in the filthy Passaic and Philip's dream when he is near death. Philip's vision, however, removes him from the world into a realm of conventional apocalypse, whereas the baptism/ drowning in "The Wanderer" welds the poet's consciousness to the actual world, "Till I felt the utter depth of its rottenness / . . . / And dropped down knowing this was me now"

(*CEP*, 11). In reality they are opposite visions, and the poems in which they occur proceed from opposite psychic impulses. To read "The Wanderer" immediately after reading the earlier work is almost to witness Keats being reborn as Whitman, and to see the pursuit of static and remote beauty give way to a passionate identification with present existence. Unlike Whitman, however, Williams could feel no joy in this identification. When he at last lost all hope of attaining the sort of perfection he was pursuing in his *Endymion* poem, the reality he accepted in its place seemed to him a tawdry exchange.

"There is not a fiercer hell than the failure in a great object," writes Keats in the preface to *Endymion*. The reader of the poem, he says, "must soon perceive great inexperience, immaturity, and every error denoting a feverish attempt, rather than a deed accomplished."[10] One might make the same assessment of Williams' attempted imitation of Keats' poem. The persistent archaisms ("clept," "sweven"), the inversions, the peculiarly Miltonic adjectives (Philip's "closeless" eyes), suggest not so much a lack of originality as an abundance of misdirected energy. Williams was trying too hard, ransacking his library for poetical effects which he then applied to his poem the way one might apply icing to a failed cake. One hesitates even to affirm that the exercise was valuable in terms of Williams' "apprenticeship." To fail in a great object for several years, to know that one is failing and yet not to be able to give it up, can do severe damage to one's sense of self. On the positive side, the poem allowed Williams to let out in disguised form some of his fantasies and psychological preoccupations. Philip is clearly an alter ego for Williams:

> A slender serious featured boy who knew
> By truth[']s sheer grace his father not at all
> But loved his mother like the breathing air. [YALC]

In "A Tragedy," the operative father figure is merely "grim," remote, and perversely possessive; in this later poem, the father moves from remoteness to active viciousness and in the end poisons everyone present at his son's wedding party, including himself. One need not conclude that William G. Williams was a vicious man or that his son thought him so. But his frequent and prolonged absences from home during Williams' boyhood, and the emotional reserve beneath his urbane exterior, could easily have provoked in Williams the desire for a covert revenge. Casting the father as the worst villain since Bluebeard would be that revenge. The female figures, on the other hand, are models of devotion and emotional warmth. Like Williams' own mother dreamily recounting stories of her romantic youth in Paris, Beatrix tells her son Philip ". . . of foreign kingdoms o'er the sea, / Of sands that shone like sheeted gold. . . ." All of this young Philip drank in with breathless delight, until he practically lived in a dream world, and saw "The actual round all golden through its mesh." No clearer confession of Mrs. Williams' influence upon her son's early aesthetic conceptions could be asked, nor any clearer indication that even at this early date Williams knew that his Keatsian poems made life unreal, filtering it through a golden "mesh."

Another female figure of importance in the poem is the eighty-year-old servant who saves Philip's life after the mass poisoning. Although she is treated only briefly, her physical appearance, her function as the hero's savior, and her witch-like knowledge of herbs and antidotes suggest that she is the prototype of the strange goddess who officiates at the poet's rites of passage in "The Wanderer." The latter figure was based in part upon the character of Williams' English grandmother, in part upon those subconscious sources from which all of Williams' superhuman female figures, from Kora to the colossal sleepmate of Paterson, ultimately spring. Most of these figures, like the old servant in this 1908 poem, serve as spiritual midwives, making possible the poet-hero's transition from death to rebirth, or more generally, from one state of consciousness to another.

When Philip "dies," his bride, mother, father, councillors, and all the wedding guests die with him. When he is miraculously revived, no world is left for him. The trappings of romance have been violently removed. He therefore flees, becomes a wanderer without memory, never realizing that what he is really trying to escape is the poem in which he finds himself. No wonder Williams hit an impasse and ultimately had to abandon the work. Having, in unconscious rebellion, obliterated the chilvalric setting and all its inhabitants, Williams found himself without a viable poetic world into which his alter ego could be reborn.

Now would have been the time for him to take another look into those free verse notebooks, for in them lay a key to his release. Instead, in May 1909, a thin booklet appeared, *Poems* by William C. Williams, signaling the poet's temporary retreat to a solution that had already proved impracticable. At twenty-five, Williams was apparently still unable to resolve the conflicting needs for spontaneous passion and aesthetic permanence except in a static and funereal realm of stop-time: "She cannot fade, though thou hast not thy bliss," as Keats expresses the impossible situation.[11]

Critics have noted that the word "new" appears twice in the book's two epigraphs (from Keats and Shakespeare), pointing ahead, they say, to the originality of Williams' later books, as well as to Pound's dictum, "Make it new." The critics seem not to have noticed that "forever" also appears twice, and that the title page, designed by Edgar, bears a strong (probably accidental) resemblance to many nineteenth-century New

England gravestones. The major difference is that, instead of
the usual lilies and orchids, Edgar bordered the page with simple daisies or misdrawn dandelions. If anything forward-look-
ing is to be found on the title page of *Poems*, it will be seen
in this simple touch.

It is possible, then, that Williams conceived of the book as
an ending rather than a beginning, as an epitaph to his youth
and to a wrongly directed apprenticeship. The fact that he
did not even try to find a commercial publisher for the book
is perhaps an indication of his doubts about the poems it contains. But the title page suggests other possibilities as well.
The common weeds and wild flowers that adorn the page are
strongly reminiscent of the designs on the cover of the first
edition of *Leaves of Grass* (1855). At the turn of the century, copies of that edition could still be found on the shelves
of secondhand book dealers. Williams need not have seen an
actual copy of that edition; there is a photograph of its cover
in Bliss Perry's book on Whitman which appeared in 1906.
Considering Williams' obsession with Whitman, it is not at
all unlikely that he saw Perry's book.[12] If so, the title page of
Poems does indeed look forward as well as backward, suggesting a Whitmanian "new" as well as the Keatsian "forever."

The "happy melodist" of the first epigraph, "forever piping
songs forever new," announces the theme of the poems themselves: the withdrawal from life into a rarified realm of imagination. The second epigraph, lines eleven and twelve of
Shakespeare's Sonnet LXXVI, apologizes for the book's old-
fashioned style. Here is the whole sonnet:

> Why is my verse so barren of new pride,
> So far from variation or quick change?
> Why with the time do I not glance aside
> To new-found methods and to compounds strange?

Why write I still all one, ever the same,
And keep invention in a noted weed,
That every word doth almost tell my name,
Showing their birth and where they did proceed?
O, know, sweet love, I always write of you,
And you and love are still my argument;
So all my best is dressing old words new,
Spending again what is already spent:
> For as the sun is daily new and old,
> So is my love still telling what is told.

Williams was later to find Shakespeare's statements on writing, including Hamlet's advice to the players, as pernicious as Eliot found Milton's influence on later generations (or as Williams found Eliot's); but that was not yet. All the Platonism of Shakespeare's sonnets is reflected in the early work of Williams.

Critics, in their haste to dismiss *Poems,* have failed to notice that the book does have a design, and a fairly complex one. The first poem is titled "Innocence" and the last, "Hymn to Perfection." The action of the book is a pilgrimage from the first to the second of these heavenly states. Far from being a miscellaneous collection, *Poems* can in fact be seen as a single, long "progress" poem. A sampling of titles along the way confirms the impression: "Innocence," "To Simplicity," ("Thee have I lost," moans the poet in line two), "The Quest of Happiness," "Love," "To My Better Self," and as the going gets rougher, "The Loneliness of Life," "The Folly of Preoccupation," "The Bewilderment of Youth," "The Bewilderment of Age," and at last "Hymn to the Spirit of Fraternal Love," and "Hymn to Perfection." The fact that the final two poems in the book are hymns suggests the threshold to which his mental journey led him.

These vaguely allegorical poems are interspersed with others which provide an accompanying seasonal progression: "June," "July," "September," "November," and "On a Proposed Trip South."[13] The last poem transports the poet back to spring by purely mechanical means, *primavera ex machina.* It is a fascinating rehearsal for later performances in which spiritual rebirth and seasonal change are obsessively intertwined. In the present book—a clumsy watch made with foreign parts, which the poet hopes to set ticking forever—the renewal is appropriately an artificial one, one which in fact is only "proposed."

In a real sense, the book is a collection of wish-fulfillments: "To in a breath's space wish the winter through / And lo, to see it fading!" as he puts it in the above poem. But paradoxically, the deepest wish he expresses is to be free of all his desires. Besides the seasonal poems and interlocked spiritual allegories, ten other poems provide useful mortar to fill in gaps and fill up pages; six of these are love poems in a pseudometaphysical mode. Only one of these, a singsong poem called "Ballad of Time and the Peasant," admits to any physical desires. It is as if only peasants can be allowed sensuality; one can't expect better from them. In fact, again and again the book expresses a frightened hostility to sex:

> We'll draw the light latch-string
> And close the door of sense. ["The Uses of Poetry"]

> Passion 'tis not, foul and gritty,
> Born one instant, instant dead. ["Love"]

> There enters no thing scatheless from the womb.
> ["The Folly of Preoccupation"]

This last from a young man who was spending his days pulling babies out of the bodies of women. Later in life, Williams was to see his poetry and his medical practice as nourishing each other; but in his anguished youth (a "hell of repression" as he called it) they seemed irreconcileable, and in each he found a refuge from the other. "The Loneliness of Life" speaks of the poet's longing to "breast this overwhelming tide, / This torrent of mortality, and stand / Glittering in sunlight on the green high land." His poetry was the green high land, the clean and clarified perspective; and of course, being the sole occupant of that land, the poet is "lonely."[14] Perfection is not sociable, and those who aspire toward it are the driven. The poet, having lost the prepubescent innocence with which the book starts, must push himself on toward its higher counterpart, perfection, which alone "calm'st my affliction."

"But imperfection clings all forms about," he admits in one of his least perfect poems ("The Folly of Preoccupation"); and the salve of noble sentiment, culminating in the Empedoclean "Hymn to Perfection," can have only temporary effect on his real afflictions. So completely self-divided was the young Williams that no reader could have guessed from his book the embroilments of his daily life. Two of the poems, "On Thinking of a Distant Friend," and "A Street Market, New York, 1908," provide a few hints. The first of these begins:

> Up stairs and stairs I climb, the final task
> Of all the day's continual duties done;
> Nor dream of aught more sweet, now hath the sun
> In cumbrous mists descended, than to bask
>
> In his fast fading light awhile . . .

The opening lines carry some suggestion of actuality, and with a little effort one can imagine Williams returning from a long day at the French Hospital and climbing to his room.

But then all sense of reality—even dream reality—is buried under piles of cotton-stuffed Romantic diction. One begins to suspect a subconscious significance to the stairs up which the poet climbs, as if to get *above* the physical realm. Ten years later, in *Kora in Hell: Improvisations*, Williams' psyche would be moving in an opposite direction: "Dig deeper *mon ami*, the rock maidens are running naked in the dark cellars" (*Imag.*, 54).

The second poem, "A Street Market, New York, 1908," begins:

> Eyes that can see,
> Oh, what a rarity!
> For many a year gone by
> I've looked and nothing seen
> But ever been
> Blind to a patent wide reality.

A hopeful beginning, and an accurate diagnosis of what is wrong with every poem in the book; but the promise of particularity is not kept in succeeding stanzas. Instead of evoking the images and raucous sounds of the street market, as Whitman would surely have done, Williams makes a mad attempt to wedge New York City itself into his Grecian urn, where "gaily sing / Slavs, Teutons, Greeks, *sweet songs forever new*" (italics mine). The importation of Keats is almost unbelievable here. Yet with Williams everything exists from the beginning, and even in these absurd lines one sees the aesthetic problem that obsessed him all his life: how to raise the commonplace to a level of distinction. The solution was not to put a gilded frame around reality; but in 1908 he didn't know that. "I discovered quite soon that it was not what I wanted, but it was all I could do. I was terribly earnest" (*IWWP*, 14).

Fortunately, there *was* something else he could do to break out of the poetic bind. As early as 1904 he writes to his mother that he has made the Mask and Wig Club; and the Medical School yearbook for 1906 shows a fine picture of Williams dressed as Polonius, and *lurking*. In April of 1907 he reports to Edgar that he has finished his second play (L). In November 1910, he tells Viola Baxter that he put on a "little play" and that it went fairly well (YALC). In January 1913, he asks her to take part in a "small play" he has written (YALC). In January 1914, he is busy translating the *Nuevo Mundo* of Lope de Vega, and says he hopes to see it on the stage (YALC). In April of that year, he tells Viola about several "playlets" he has in his mind to write (YALC). His insistence on using diminutives when talking about his dramatic efforts should not fool anyone into thinking he wasn't serious. One of his few statements about the plays he was writing at this time appears at the end of an unpublished letter to Viola Baxter, October 15, 1911. Its tone suggests a methodical determination: "My dramatic attempts are slowly but surely, I believe, rounding into a more and more complete semblance of the desired form. I devote a great deal of time to this and mean to succeed" (YALC).

None of these early plays has been published, and only one is known to have survived. With Williams' help, Vivienne Koch located several of them in the mid-forties, and she discusses them at length in her pathfinding work on the poet.[15] She has since died, and the plays have disappeared. All efforts to locate them have been unsuccessful. Fortunately, her discussions are fairly detailed and include sizable quotations. Koch eschews footnotes and sometimes neglects to verify dates, but it appears that the one-act play "A September Afternoon" was written in the spring of 1909, toward the end of Williams' internship. Like his poetry at this time, the play was static in tone, and the dialogue, according to Koch, "while striving for realism, sounds as if the young playwright were reading Synge and the Irish 'folk' writers. . . . The rhythm and the inverted syntax of the following is illustrative: 'For the love of God come home, you crazy boy! Come home! It's this we've been fearing the two weeks now they've been camping beyond the hills' " (148). Synge or Yeats are possible influences at this time (Williams took a course in 1909 in contemporary English drama), but the accidental brogue could also be accounted for simply in terms of his efforts to write that he considered poetic drama (lots of anapests, few connectives).

This play and another called "Plums," from about the same period, are set at the beginning of the American Revolution. The first, says Koch, is a "literary dramatized argument" between a brother and sister over the merits of risking one's neck for "a lot of fools fighting over a cow." The brother finally does join the offstage war and is fatally wounded. The second play presents "the point of view of the landowner whose intelligence and cultivation [have] brought prosperity and eminence to the Hudson valley and who, by aristocratic allegiances as well as self-interest, is with the British. The Yankees, represented by two plum-stealing soldiers, are shown as crass, marauding, and unperceptive of the true quality of the land they would 'free' " (148). Some years later, Williams himself became a plum-stealer in his poem "This Is Just To Say"; but in these early plays he has not given his unequivocal allegiance to the rebels.

A third play mentioned by Koch, "Sauerkraut to the Cultured: A Nieu Amsterdam Comedy," set in 1680, does suggest the beginnings of such an allegiance. The protagonist, an old burgher named Johan Friedrich Bach, father of a marriageable daughter, speaks in the downright manner of Samuel Johnson: "You new ones in the city are so busy improving, that you never have time to learn, but I live by profession evenly. All your misery comes from mixing levels. As long as men keep to their levels all is happiness but if a man live at knee level and pretend to the chin level his end is fixed. I, sir, live a little above the knee" (150). The distrust of schemes for improving human life, and the assumption of the existence of inherent social levels, are more Johnsonian and aristocratic than they are American. But the play as a whole asserts the dignity and even beauty of "knee-level" life, when it does not make itself ridiculous by social pretensions. Miss Koch is probably right to see in Johan's speech a prefiguration of Williams' later celebrations of the local and the common. One might even view the speech as Williams' answer to Pound, who was already beckoning from Europe. Williams, severely self-divided and always to remain so, was busy digging roots for himself in American history, working up the courage to "live by profession evenly" and anonymously, planting himself (Pound would say, burying himself) as firmly as he could in a soil to which his parents were foreigners. To make biographical inferences is to extrapolate a great deal from scraps of a play that may no longer even exist,[16] but it is at least suggestive that all these "lost" plays, and others mentioned in the *Autobiography*, deal with American history.

If these early plays are never recovered, our knowledge of Williams' early theatrical abilities—above all, the ability (for which he later became famous) to capture the nuances of common speech—will remain slight. But there has been one stroke of luck. Williams' son, Dr. William Eric Williams, has allowed me access to a medical file in use between the years 1908 and 1911. The drawer of four-by-six-inch cards, marked

"GENERAL INDEX," is divided into two alphabetical listings. The one in the front half of the drawer lists diseases and remedies, as well as infractions of the health code noted during his 1910–1911 tenure as local school inspector ("Desks   3 too h.   4 too low. Heat good, vent. good   pupils alert.   glare of light.   Floors"). The second alphabetical listing occupies the rest of the drawer and details the more personal concerns that were constantly in the back of his mind. Under "I" in this second section of the file, Williams has a listing for "Index," in which he explains his reasons for keeping such a file: "Index acquired April 21 – '08   It seems an advantageous way to retain impressions, fleeting ideas and exact facts for easy future reference and as these are expected to be of some value this system has been adoptd. No definite class of data to be collected. The plan to be general." Among other intriguing material in this back section of the index ("Flowers Observed, Wild, in & about Rutherford," 1908–1909; "Books to be read," 1908–1910), there are notes and scraps of dialogue for at least nine plays, none of them mentioned elsewhere. Whether any of these plays was ever finished and performed is impossible to tell from the rough notes that remain.

In addition to the preliminary outlines of plays, this second alphabetical listing contains twenty-five cards (twenty of them written on both sides) under the heading "Contemporary Eng. Drama." Their presence is no doubt explained by a passage in the *Autobiography* describing his 1909 trip to Leipzig to study medicine: "To offset the monotony of my medical work (I was getting along pretty well with the German by that time) I took a course in modern British Drama at the university, but I didn't realize it would be in English until I went to the first class" (111). From the evidence provided by the file cards, the course began with the 1820's, gave considerable emphasis to Oscar Wilde and George Bernard Shaw, and ended with "W. B. Yeats poet & dramatist. . . . The hero at war with all worldly institutions   We must destroy the world."

Williams' notes on his own plays are for the most part sketchy and quite preliminary. One play sometimes seems to be reincarnated into the next, with different characters and setting, but with a similar theme and plot. The first play mentioned in the file is called "The Artificial Family." It requires three characters: She, He, and The Baby. Here is Williams' synopsis: "Her sister dies a week after her husband & beque[a]thes to her a boy 1 week old. For years He has been after She,   but She has refused him. The baby grows expensive. So the She finally accept[s] He. Quite a family & happy too."

A scribbled envelope stuck into the file at this point changes and complicates the plot. Apparently, instead of dying, the first husband has sneaked off to New York (act 1). The determined admirer marries the woman in his absence (act 2); but in act 3 they quarrel and the first husband is brought back by a "revengeful constable" who is himself in love with the woman. The constable's idea is to "thwart his rival," the second husband, by bringing back the first; but in the end he himself "is thwarted by their gratitude" (apparently the gratitude of the woman and the first husband, who have been reunited). As a light romantic comedy it might have some amusing possibilities.

Another three index cards outline yet a third permutation of the same situation. The play is called "A Quaker Soak." In it, Jordan Pennypacker, James Cummings, and Job Grammercy—Quakers of three different sects—resolve their romantic differences over Job's wife, Esther. Pennypacker and

Cummings try to get Job drunk in order to woo his wife without interference, but Job is not as drunk as he seems. He "comes to after he learns wife does not love him. She is surprised. Both are delighted when they find neither loves the other. They shake hands & congratulate each other & agree to help each other   she to get *him* [Cummings] + husb. to get square" with the other Quaker for having made him sick with bad liquor. Job pretends he is dying. The suitor who has been plying him with liquor is afraid that he has poisoned him and flees. Then Job himself leaves for New York, and Esther gets her lover.

But on the next card Williams expresses apparent dissatisfaction with this resolution: there is too much "good natured tolerance," "stagnation," and "do nothingism" in it. He proposes to establish this tone of stagnation and then to break it, as "Shem [James Cummings] in a passion (serious) drives the others out & claims her. Settles all difficulties, clears atmosphere."

Williams' use of a decisive act with which to clear the atmosphere reflects more than his sense of the theatrical. As he said later about his poetic practice: "Having once taken the plunge the situation that preceded it becomes obsolete which a moment before was alive with malignant rigidities" (*Imag.*, 51). The same is true on a biographical level, as Chapter Two will indicate. In 1909, Williams lost at love and almost immediately proposed to the sister of the girl he had been in love with. That sudden decision, seemingly arbitrary, turned out to be one of the most fortunate he ever made. The decisive actions of the determined lover in "The Artificial Family" and of the passionate Quaker in "A Quaker Soak" were set down perhaps only a few months after Williams had faced a similar situation.

Throughout these notes for projected plays, Williams seems to be performing dances in the air over the difficult facts of his own life. Between 1909 and 1912, he was living in that state of emotional suspension known as being engaged. He had plenty of opportunity to ponder the dangers of marriage and the compromises he might have to make to support a family. One card, marked "Play," presents, not a plot, but a problem: "A man has lived by the true standard & when pressed tries to change to the practical. There is no help   as high as you chose on that level you will be judged. No going back   only forward can win." What the "true standard" might be only Williams, or Williams' mother, would know. But there is no doubt that a young poet's decision to marry and raise a family entails a "change to the practical."

It is a problem elaborated with different emphasis in "Lost Wealth," a projected play which fills twelve cards. The play was to be a tragedy, in which a father who has sacrificed his own poetic instincts in order to become financially successful sinks into lethargic misery as the eventual result. Only his stiff pride remains intact. His grown daughter, just returned from a conservatory in Europe, feels her high spirits being dragged down by her father's chronic despondency. His son, a young doctor, has just been suspended from his position at a hospital. The father's only response to the situation is to offer to use his influence to "fix it up" for his son. But the son, who has been looking for guidance, not for lessons in expediency, is disillusioned; he toys with the idea of going out West to start over.

The drama gets sudsier, but what is interesting is the way Williams reconstitutes the personal relationships of his own life. In a sort of meditative revery, Williams trades parents with his fiancée, becomes (perhaps for reasons of emotional safety) the brother of the girl he had in real life been in love with, and divides his own anxieties equally between himself (as the Young Doctor) and the tortured and ineffectual father.

Another play, "Sartor," which occupies eleven cards in the index, continues the biographical revery in a German setting. *Sartor Resartus*, upon which the play is loosely based, is Carlyle's own spiritual autobiography. In it, Carlyle sets forth his theory of the individual's relationship to a universe permeated by the "divine idea"—a relationship to be developed through renunciation and work. Williams was already learning something about renunciation and work and perhaps saw in the character of Diogenes Teufelsdröckh certain analogies to himself. He may have been even more attracted by the dichotomy that Carlyle's hero sets up between the conscious mind (the realm of manufacture) and the unconscious mind (the realm of creation). The same duality plagued and propelled Williams' own work all his life.

Although the scraps of dialogue that remain suggest an attempt at realistic conversation, the characters all seem to have an archetypal rather than a sociological reality:

Youth: a magnificent barbarian   a vandal, unspoiled by intellect.
Teuf: a powerful physique, wrecked by intellect & made useless.
Host: a little man
Hostess: a vigorous, keen & beautiful but ignorant woman.
Daughter: *big*, vigorous, primitive, a young goddess the antithesis of dainty.

The plot is not clearly outlined, but one gathers that the daughter is in love with the beautiful youth and that Teufelsdröckh wants to steer her into marriage with someone else, a slightly built baron with a keen intellect and "rotten ancestry." "It is a fight bet. Teuf. & this boy his pupil to perpetuate the strain"—a symbolic fight for survival involving two extreme human possibilities: the noble and passionate savage and the calculating intellectual. One can see in this conflict a projection of the conflict of interest Williams apparently felt in himself: poet versus scientist, instinct versus thought. Significantly, the woman is the determining factor. Whoever wins this earth goddess, this Kora, will have the strength to be victorious. Williams always mythologized women, even while he extracted infants from their bleeding bodies. As he says in the *Autobiography*, "Men have given the direction to my life and women have always supplied the energy" (55). When this daughter/goddess is prevented, through the machinations of Teufelsdröckh, from meeting her lover, she "tears around like a wild animal in all her power and beauty." For equivalent descriptions of primal mother-consciousness one must turn to Erich Neumann, Robert Graves, or Robert Bly.

There is something of the quality of exorcism and of invocation in this writing. Williams is struggling to deal with his psychological difficulties by externalizing them and by exercising fictive control over them. One suspects that the plays also served another function, that of breaking the artistic isolation into which Williams was forced by his relentlessly idealistic poetry. He was "terribly earnest" about the poetry and terribly lonely in the rarified world he created. By getting his brother and Flossie and various Rutherford acquaintances together to put on plays, he was able for an evening to view art as socially unifying, rather than alienating. The same impulse lies behind later poems in which Williams addresses "my townspeople."

Writing the plays helped him to go on writing the poetry; it may even have helped to bring the poetry down toward time and place and people. But facile explanations of literary evolution must be avoided, particularly in the case of Williams, in whom a number of opposite tendencies, literary and psychological, existed from the beginning. He was always a social creature and always a little remote; he wrote some of his earliest poems in a "late" style; his obsession with America and American behavior surfaced at a time when his dependence on received "European" literary forms was most abject; and so on. Looking at Williams' life at this time, one senses that he is all there already, though spiritually *in ovo;* nothing needs to be "added" to his life at a later time. The gestation was a long one, uncommonly so, but he was already beginning the astonishing series of transformations and reembodiments that would continue all his life, leaving bewildered critics to pick up the books he left behind.

CHAPTER TWO

Transition Years, 1910–1917

Williams' feeling about his own performance in *Poems* is perhaps best captured in a passage near the end of his last novel, *The Build-Up:*

> Sometimes Charlie Bishop would read her his poems, bitterly, defiantly, in a harsh voice.
> "Why do you write like that?" she would ask him, puzzled. "Your first little book was beautiful."
> "It stank," he said bitterly. "I was a fool ever to have let it be printed."
> "No it wasn't," said Lottie. "I loved it."
> "It just shows your ignorance."
> "And you wrote me such a nice sentiment in it." He ground his teeth. "But these things, you are making fun of yourself. I don't think a poem, to be a poem, should use ugly words, dirty words, vulgar. . . . A poem should be beautiful. And you can write beautifully. But you seem to want to spoil everything. Why is that?"
> He would laugh to himself sardonically and change the subject. "I don't understand you," she would say.   [238]

It is an extreme reaction, suggesting a deep disillusionment not just with his own work but equally with the ideal of poetic beauty that underlay it. "We have discarded beauty," he said simply, some years later (*SE,* 75). In mid-1909, he had not discarded it, but he had begun to suspect it. If the above

scene actually took place, and there is no reason to assume it
didn't, it may have happened some time after Williams had
received Pound's letter of May 21 ("Great art it is not," was
one of the kinder phrases Pound used to describe *Poems*), and
before Williams' July departure for Germany to continue his
medical studies. The intervening months were a time of great
emotional upheaval for Williams. Apparently, he and his
brother Edgar were in love with the same girl, Florence Her-
man's sister, Charlotte, and Edgar won. " 'Fine,' said Charlie
[that is, Williams] and then, disgracefully, he flung his arms
about his brother's neck and went mad" (259). A few days
later he proposed to Florence. "He was obviously in a disturbed mental state" (261).[1] But somehow he knew that, in
shifting his allegiance from the exotic, artistic Lottie to the
more practical Flossie, he was making a choice that carried
implications for later choices. His verse would begin to reflect a preference for sparrows rather than nightingales, bread
rather than caviar, the spirit of Whitman (America) rather
than the spirit of Keats (Europe). Certainly no one would
claim that his choice of one woman over another was the
cause of the revolution in Williams' aesthetic. But his mind
never lost its mythical turn, and possibly he saw in these two
very different sisters an embodiment of his own divided
psyche.

The description in *The Build-Up* of "Charlie's" relationship with Flossie sounds very much like some of Williams'
later formulations of an American aesthetic: "It was not an
adulteration, not a leftover from her sister's bouquet. It was a
vivid, living thing—of a new sort" (263). But this new thing
(the implicit image is that of a flower, one not likely to be
found in Lottie's bouquet) had no "heavenly birth," but as-
cended out of darkness, out of the dirt. As he put it on the

previous page: "He would never go back. Never. There is a
sort of love, not romantic love, but a love that with daring
can be made difficultly to blossom. It is founded on passion,
a dark sort of passion, but it is founded on passion, a passion
of despair, as all life is despair" (262). Williams' feelings
about his future wife are strangely disturbing, as if they'd
been purchased at a drastic price. Again there is the implicit
flower imagery, which surfaces almost always when Williams
is speaking of his deepest self. The ambiguous resonance of
the statement may best be understood when compared with
an equally cryptic statement in a letter to Marianne Moore,
concerning the "inner security" of his work: "It is something
which occurred once when I was about twenty, a sudden res-
ignation to existence, a despair—if you wish to call it that, but
a despair which made everything a unit and at the same time
a part of myself. I suppose it might be called a sort of nameless religious experience. I resigned, I gave up." Toward the
end of that same letter he says, "Things have no names for
me. . . . As a reward for this anonymity I feel as much a
part of things as trees and stones. Heaven seems frankly impossible. I am damned as I succeed. I have no particular hope
save to repair, to rescue, to complete" (*SL*, 147). One may
conjecture that Williams' chronology in this extraordinary
passage is not quite accurate; that the experience he speaks of
took place not at "about twenty," but at about twenty-five,
just before he left for Germany to continue his medical studies. Until then he was extremely naive, for all his experience
interning in hospitals. His "despair"—stemming in part from
the discrepancy between his ideals of moral and artistic perfection and his sense of his own unworthiness—continued to
grow, but he had not yet experienced that "sudden resigna-
tion to existence" which he speaks of in the letter to Mari-

anne Moore. For one thing, he was still tinkering with his *Endymion* imitation. "I'd find somewhere in that 'primeval forest' my theme for the week-end, go back to Rutherford, listen to Charlotte (Flossie's older sister) play Chopin and retreat to my room at home to compose" (*Auto.*, 60). The connection between Charlotte's playing and Williams' romantic poeticizing may be coincidental, but their juxtaposition is suggestive. At any rate, "in disgust, one day [and here again one might conjecture a particular day in that spring of 1909], perhaps through impatience with my 'heroics,' I took the voluminous script, and running downstairs before I should begin to 'think,' opened the furnace door and in with it!" (*Auto.*, 60).

Of course, Williams was not by this act immediately freed of his limitations, emotional or artistic, and the "nameless religious experience" was probably yet to come; but something was completed and something was released. "I have never been able to make out quite what happened at that time, for something profound did happen, something moving and final" (*Auto.*, 55). Williams' own recurrent imagery suggests that he had died and was waiting for a new birth, the first of several spiritual reincarnations he was to put himself through during his life. "It must change; it must reappear in another form, to remain permanent. It is the image of the Phoenix. To stop the flames that destroy the old nest prevents the rebirth of the bird itself" (*SE*, 208).

Change, continual and cyclical, was to characterize Williams' next ten years, just as stasis had characterized the preceding ten. Once his severe inhibitions toward the world and toward poetry itself began breaking down, things began happening very quickly: Europe in late 1909 and 1910, marriage in 1912, publication of his second book and the start of private practice in 1913, involvement in avant-garde artistic and literary circles from 1913 on, association with the magazine *Others* from 1915 to 1919, publication of *Al Que Quiere!* in late 1917. In tracing these transition years, one's best hope is to proceed chronologically, trying to keep sight of the man in the swirl of events.

In early summer, 1909, as he prepared to leave for Europe, Williams was probably more concerned with what he was putting behind him than with what lay ahead. After all, he had recently been forced to admit to failure in both poetry and love. In mid-July, his mind in a state of great turbulence, he left. To Pound's disgust, he set sail for Leipzig, not London, partly because of the reputation of Leipzig's medical programs, and partly, he later admits, because he had been in love with a "concert pianist who had spent three years there at the Conservatory" (*Auto.*, 109). The unnamed pianist is Flossie's sister Charlotte. Williams, recently engaged to Florence, was still sniffing out the cold trail of Charlotte's secret and romantic past. "How easy to slip / into the old mode," he says in another context, "how hard to / cling firmly to the advance" (*Imag.*, 103). Yet he was already committed to the advance, however longingly he might continue to gaze into the past. The result was predictable:

I wrote nothing, or very little. I was looking for a short form which would not be a sonnet. Even then I detested sonnets. I had devised a thing with an *abba bccb caac* scheme in iambic pentameters. One day I decided to take a solitary trip out to Grimma, near Leipzig, to see the remains of the nunnery where Katherina von Bora, Luther's bride, once lived. It was a romantic holiday, horribly sentimental in its implications—but I shall never forget it. I wrote something about that but that was all. [*Auto.*, 110]

In the Lockwood Library there are two short manuscripts, one marked "Two Sonnets: 1909," and the other, "Poems, 1910–1912," six short poems in all, representing almost the only work Williams wished to preserve from the years immediately preceding his marriage. One of them, "The Wartburg," is undoubtedly the poem he wrote after the "horribly sentimental" excursion to Grimma. It was eventually published in the *Little Review* in 1926, and reprinted by John Thirlwall in *New Directions 16* (1957). The versions of it which appear, under different titles, in the two Lockwood manuscripts differ not only from each other, but also from the published version. Unfortunately, all manuscripts of poems from 1909 and before are restricted; it is therefore not possible to reproduce the first manuscript, which contains, besides "The Wartburg," a highly symmetrical poem called "San Marco," whose mellifluous diction and interweaving rhymes convey Williams' confession of discomfort at finding himself in the midst of such a poem. As he says in the *Autobiography* (49), "I . . . looked at my more or less stumpy fingers and smiled. An esthete, huh? Some esthete."

Here is the text of the second manuscript:

Poems, 1910–1912

And Thus With All Praise:
  Wonderful creatures!
  Why must I call you bride and mother?
  Curst be the idle mockery and fashion lie of such
    names!
  Be delight unto me rather!

  Joy at the encounter!
  Sorrow at the ends of things!
  Be to me deeds of compassion:
  Have these for name, none other.

Martin and Katharine:

> Alone today I mounted that steep hill
> On which the Wartburg stands. Here Luther dwelt
> [In] a small room one year through, here he spelt
> The German Bible out by God's great will.
>
> The birds piped ti-ti-tu, and as I went
> I thought how Katharine of Bora knelt
> In Grimma, idle she, waiting to melt
> Her surpliced heart in folds less straitly meant.
>
> As now, it was March then: lo, he'll fulfill
> Today his mighty task! Sing for content
> Ye birds! Pipe now, for now 'tis love's wing's bent!
> Work sleeps: love wakes: sing and the glad air thrill!

Ah, Les Femmes:

> Let her be maid or mistress!
> Let her be a brown peasant!
> Let her be pale of confinement
> Holy or hellish!
> Let her be even black:
> So she be feminine, sexed of the heart,
> It matters nothing for form or figure
> When her eyes speak from the heart
> Greeting me
> There is no vilest humor:
> No terror: no confusion
> Of the any colored discords which beset me
> But that moment is made music for her greeting.

The Good:

> Your abusive letter, dear, corrodes my lips:
> I am burned sweeter than ever your kisses burnt me,
> By which, lo, how marvelously swift time slips
> Beneath us and worth may lie neglected till too late!

What You Will:

> Make up your mind, or not, to take and give with me;
> Live with me or do not live with me
> And for God's sake cut it sharp, either way,
> But let's not talk of love at this late day.

One is immediately struck by the way the poems are brought together in groups, as if to protect them from the necessity of standing or falling on their own. Young writers often feel there is something impressive in offering a "suite" of poems, such as Williams himself offered in his first book. The poem about Luther, which appears both in "Two Sonnets: 1909" and in "Poems, 1910–1912," is so greatly affected by the force of context that Williams apparently felt compelled to change the title to reflect the difference in emphasis. In the first group, form and geographical setting are the unifying elements, thus the title, "The Wartburg." In the second group, the theme is love, and the arrangement suggests a progression from naive idealism to disillusionment, thus the more personal "Martin and Katharine."

One notices, too, an awkwardness in Williams' efforts to return to the free verse forms with which he began his career. Recognizing the inevitability of failure in any competition with a real "esthete," such as Keats, and spurred by Pound's success in looser forms, Williams began looking for ways to open up his verse. Dactyls replace some of the iambs, and feminine slant rhymes (creatures/mother/rather/encounter/ other) replace the perfect end rhymes. The rhetoric, which was always rather exclamatory, is no longer directed at personified abstractions, but at particular people ("Make up your mind, or not," and so forth), suggesting some of Donne's expostulations to his mistress or Pound's to his songs.

But these are all half-measures; none of the poems resulting from them has the clean quiet shock value of the enjambment that concludes the first poem Williams wrote: "driven by fierce flying / rain." He seemed unable to admit that a decade of apprenticeship to the craft of sonnet-making had taught him virtually nothing, except what to avoid. But he didn't know *how* to avoid the tricks he had so painfully learned and seemed uncertain what would be left if he erased the warm blur of alliteration or the certitudes of a preexistent pattern. In the first prose section of *Spring and All*, written a decade after the above poems, Williams answers the objections of those who view his latest work as "positively repellent," and "heartlessly cruel": "Perhaps this noble apostrophe [the objections of Williams' critics] means something terrible for me, I am not certain, but for the moment I interpret it to say: 'You have robbed me. God, I am naked. What shall I do?' —By it they mean that when I have suffered (provided I have not done so as yet) I too shall run for cover" (*Imag.*, 88–89). To follow Williams' career from 1912 to 1918 is to witness an agonizing process of cultural divestment, an unlearning process leading to the release of Kora's primal scream. In the Lockwood manuscript poems we see him removing his hat.

A year later, in 1913, Williams was married and had begun his practice, and Flossie was pregnant. They had also undertaken to buy a house of their own, 9 Ridge Road, Rutherford, New Jersey, a few blocks from the house where Williams had been born. Perhaps it was his impending thirtieth birthday that prompted him suddenly to accept the responsibilities which he had put off for several years. But now he was ready to "grip down and begin to awaken." A package arrived from Elkin Mathews, Pound's English publisher, containing copies of *The Tempers*, Williams' first commercially published volume.

Pound's friendly notice of the book in *The New Free-woman* (London, December 1, 1913), captures precisely the change of direction in Williams' work: "He makes a bold effort to express himself directly and convinces one that the emotions expressed are veritably his own[;] wherever he shows traces of reading, it would seem to be a snare against which he struggles, rather than a support to lean upon. It is this that gives one hope for his future work." Pound might never have made this uncharacteristic remark about reading had Williams been raised on Provençal poets rather than Pal-grave's *Golden Treasury*. In fact, two major literary influ-ences work to mitigate the originality of *The Tempers;* the first is Spanish poetry, particularly the great fifteenth-century cycle, *El Romancero,* and the second, the work of Ezra Pound himself.

Williams soon recognized that his Spanish translations were unsuccessful, and he never allowed them to be reprinted. But the literature meant enough to him to prompt him to trans-late some of the same poems again—again unsuccessfully, but less disastrously so—for his 1936 volume, *Adam and Eve and the City*. The shift from the preoccupation with Keats to an enchantment with the traditional *épico-lírico* poetry of Spain was for Williams a step in the right direction. In the first place, the poetry is not "high-brow"; it is emotional and un-pretentious, and suited well Williams' new mood of direct-ness and conviction. Yet this Spanish influence helped at the same time to make *The Tempers* a secret and devious book. Between the two bland William's of his name there lurks a Carlos, a "dark Spanish beauty," as the 1906 Medical School yearbook, *The 'Scope,* called Williams (p. 76). It is an evidence of Williams' own sense of his name's meaning that in several prose pieces, as well as in the first draft of *A Voyage to Pagany,* he refers to his alter ego as "Evan Dionysius Evans." His Spanish heritage seemed to represent to him that streak of wildness, of Dionysian abandon, which his poetry so much needed, and which Williams so much feared. Like Lawrence, Williams looked to the heavily Catholic cultures of Spain, Mexico, and Latin America, not for Christian symbology, but for images of paganism—perhaps because he identified with Spanish peasantry rather than with Spanish aristocracy. Peasants seemed to him close to earth and thus to the earth mothers of paganism. There are several revealing pages in the *Autobiography* about his one brief visit to Spain. He stopped there just before he returned home to get married and start his medical practice (and incidentally to begin translating *El Romancero*):

In Seville they were having a carnival, the streets were crowded. I saw one marvelous kid, she couldn't have been more than fifteen, doing the fandango on the stage of a little booth, with an enthusiastic crowd in front of her. . . . Had I had the nerve or the insanity to follow the little whore who waved her buttocks at me near the plaza that evening, I don't know where I might not have landed in this world or out of it. But I didn't, and so I am a writer. [122]

Dionysus remained within bounds, held tightly by his guards, William and Williams.

It may be impossible ever to understand what Williams' Spanish heritage really signified for him. His statements on the subject (such as "Spanish still seems to me synonymous with romantic"—*IWWP,* 17) are tantalizing without being informative. Certainly, his feelings about things Spanish are closely related to his feelings about his Spanish-speaking mother and, by extension, all women.

Like *Poems*, then, *The Tempers* is a "secret" book, dedicated to the Carlos in the poet's nature. Literally, it *was* dedicated to a Carlos, to his uncle Carlos Hoheb, a surgeon practicing in Puerto Rico, Haiti, and Panama. This uncle, whom Williams may not have known well at all, may have been accorded the honor of a dedication less for what he was than for what he represented: the whole man Williams wanted to become, in whom Heaven and Hell, Apollo and Dionysus, scientist and poet, German and Spaniard are finally reconciled.

Many of the poems in this collection are derivative, but it would be misleading to conclude with Breslin that Williams sought merely "to provide conventional subjects with new verbal finish," or that "his practice, while often deliberately rougher than in 1909, still equated art with rhetorical polish rather than self-expression."[2] Breslin's analysis of the book is generally brilliant, particularly in defining Williams' ambivalence toward the unavoidable influence of Pound, but his discussion fails to mention the most striking aspect of the book: Williams' creation of private myths through which covertly to express his strong but inhibited sensuality.

"Mother of flames," he begins one poem, "The men that went ahunting / Are asleep in the snow drifts" (*CEP*, 22). After the suffocated contortions of *Poems*, lines like these should evoke at least mild applause. Possibly Williams might better have written "hunting" instead of "ahunting," but even that archaism is defensible, creating a "baby bunting" nursery-rhyme effect that half harmonizes, half contrasts with the meaning. Best of all, the lines are alive and mobile. The images, some of them quite striking, resist immediate paraphrase; they do not "stand for" some obvious moral quality. In the worst poems of the book, this "senselessness" is mere obscurity, that "judicious involvement of the meaning" about which Williams had preached to his brother back in his days at Penn. But in the better ones, the images evoke genuine mysteries:

> The young wives have fallen asleep
> With wet hair . . .   [*CEP*, 22]

or

> From your tents by the sea
> Come play with us: it is forbidden!   [*CEP*, 20]

Most mysterious are lines from a poem written at about this same time, but not included in *The Tempers:*

> Give me one little flame,
> one!
> that I may bind it
> protectingly about the wrist
> of him that flung me here,
> here upon the very center!   [*CEP*, 24]

The voice in the above poem ("The Appeal") is that of a crimson salamander, doubtless a servant of the "mother of flames" in the earlier poem ("Crude Lament"). A number of fire spirits hover in and about *The Tempers*, suggesting a pagan world of magic, myth, terror, fate. One such spirit appears in "The Ordeal" and is instructed, presumably by the Mother, to save the poet from being "dismanned" by the "fire roots that circle him." She commands her servant to quench the flames and to "bring him home, / O crimson salamander, / That I may see he is unchanged with burning" (*CEP*, 23).

The poem is unsuccessful because it is too heavily plotted to be effective or even comprehensible. But it does seem to contain a clue to the book's title. The poet, like a weapon, is being "tempered" in various experiential fires until he is hard enough to be "unchanged with burning."

Connotations of sexual passion are inescapable and perhaps primary, but other sorts of fire are involved as well. The years of artistic apprenticeship were a kind of trial by fire for Williams. And his decision to throw himself into the world, to take on the responsibilities of marriage, ownership, fatherhood, medical practice, helped weld his artistic and psychological allegiance to the cult of experience rather than to the elite sect of distanced contemplation and withdrawal ("Up stairs and stairs I climb"). No doubt Williams was helped in this shift of allegiance by having witnessed the Paterson silk strike of 1913, described a year later in "The Wanderer," and by a new reading of Whitman's *Leaves of Grass* (Flossie gave him a copy in 1913). These too were fires.

In any case, *The Tempers* is a proving ground for a more competent and confident Williams. As he wrote later, "Having once taken the plunge the situation that preceded it becomes obsolete which a moment before was alive with malignant rigidities" (*Imag.*, 51). The statement is fascinating but in a sense misleading, for the rigidities in his poetry were not overcome in a moment or in a year. The irksome falseheartiness of "The Fool's Song," for instance ("Sing merrily, Truth: I tried to put / Truth in a cage! / Heigh-ho! Truth in a cage"), descends from the equally unfortunate "Ballad of Time and the Peasant" in *Poems* ("Old Time was sitting in the sun, / Sing hey for father Time!"). Both apparently derive from Elizabethan songs; for example, the Fool's song in *King Lear*, beginning, "He that has and a little tiny wit— /

With hey, ho, the wind and the rain." It cannot be denied that at times Williams is insufferable.

He is particularly so on those occasions when he chooses to think of himself as a Shakespearean Fool, simple and a little bit crazy. In part, the pose seems to function as a protection against Pound's overbearing sophistication; in part it seems to gratify the need to view himself as a simple man, his hands calloused, in contact with the physical world. Speaking of "Postlude," one of the better poems in the book, H. D. wrote to Williams: "When you speak *direct* [you] are a poet. I feel in the hey-ding-ding touch running through your poem a derivative tendency which, to me, is not *you*—not your very self" (*Imag.*, 13). The odd thing is that his "very self" was, or could be, simple, and at times in his life he almost cultivated insanity. The falsity of his occasional "fool's songs" comes from the fact that he is borrowing, archaic diction and all, a literary simplicity and a literary craziness.

Pound, too, had his reservations, even while he was persuading Elkin Mathews to publish *The Tempers*. In an unpublished letter postmarked "26 May 13," he writes to Williams, "E. M. wants your Coroners Children, which I used to revive his spirits when he moaned over one of your worst and more pseudo philosophic pieces" (L). Here is the poem that revived Williams' first publisher:

> The coroner's merry little children
>> Have such twinkling brown eyes.
> Their father is not of gay men
>> And their mother jocular in no wise,
> Yet the coroner's merry little children
>> Laugh so easily.
>
> They laugh because they prosper.
>> Fruit for them is upon all branches.

> Lo! how they jibe at loss, for
> Kind heaven fills their little paunches!
> It's the coroner's merry, merry children
> Who laugh so easily.   [*CEP*, 30]

The ostentatious unpretentiousness of the piece makes the tone seem forced, and the poet's too obvious relish in distinguishing between the dour coroner and the merry children embarrasses the reader. Yet the poem represents a real advance over anything in the first book. Instead of hymns to perfection and odes to innocence, we are given an actual observation, lyricized though it may be. The poem provides one of the first poetic evidences—beyond some silly poeticizing about toothbrushes in an early letter to Viola Baxter—of Williams' love for seizing on some small obscure thing and holding it up to the light. A decade later, in poems about the broken pieces of a green bottle or a red wheelbarrow glazed with rain water, Williams captures what might be called the luminosity of the actual. The little poem about the coroner's children achieves nothing like that clarity, but in it Williams signifies that he is willing to look low instead of high for his subject matter, and that he is able to enjoy situational perversities without indulging in moral judgments.

In a way there *is* a judgment, one in favor of willfulness and defiance. The obscurities of the book, which seem at times to function as protective camouflage, do not completely hide the naughty wink. "Come play with us: it is forbidden!" If *Poems* was an obedient book, *The Tempers* is a naughty one.

Another advance, the loosening up of Williams' clogged rhetoric, must be credited to the influence of Pound. A group of Pound's poems published in *Poetry*, April 1913, contains some of his characteristic iconoclasms about his own work, spoken in simple exclamatory language:

> Ruffle the skirts of prudes,
>   speak of their knees and ankles,
> But, above all, go to practical people—
>   go! jangle their door-bells!
> Say that you do no work
>   and that you will live forever.

The insolence of such writing was too refreshing not to be contagious, and Williams was eager to catch it. Although he was still capable, in the Spanish translations particularly, of painful verbal contortions ("Who thee lameth he also me lameth"), in other poems he was able to employ forthright rhetoric to declare his independence from his own inhibitions. The following lines are from "Con Brio":

> But, by the god of blood, what else is it that has deterred
> Us all from an out and out defiance of fear
> But this same perdamnable miserliness,
> Which cries about our necks how we shall have less and
>   less
> Than we have now if we spend too wantonly?
> Bah, this sort of slither is below contempt!
> In the same vein we should have apple trees exempt
> From bearing anything but pink blossoms all the year,
> Fixed permanent lest their bellies wax unseemly, and the
>   dear
> Innocent days of them be wasted quite.   [CEP, 31]

The martial stridency of tone, not uncommon in Pound's work, suggests bravado rather than conviction. Although Williams liked to think that the breaking down of inhibitions, sexual or literary, can take place in a moment—as quickly as his switch in attachment from Lottie to Flossie—it was actually several years before he hit squarely on his own style, in writing and in life. He could not have done it without help.

Bram Dijkstra's fine book, *The Hieroglyphics of a New Speech*,[3] indicates the extent of Williams' insufficiently acknowledged debt to the revolution in the visual arts led in America by Alfred Stieglitz and his group at "291." Stieglitz opened his "Little Galleries of the Photo-Secession" as early as 1905, and by the end of 1907 had begun exhibiting drawings as well as photographs. In 1908 he showed Matisse and Rodin, in 1909 Lautrec, Marin, and Hartley, in 1910 Rousseau, and in 1911 Cézanne and Picasso—in each case the first comprehensive showing of the artist's work in the United States.[4] In 1912, he devoted an entire issue of *Camera Work* to Gertrude Stein's essays on the works of Picasso and Matisse. If Williams missed the exhibitions (he claims, perhaps disingenuously, that he did not know Stieglitz until 1915), he is unlikely to have missed the Stein issue of Stieglitz's notorious magazine. Charles Demuth, Williams' close friend since 1903, would surely have pressed a copy into his hands.

In any case, when the Armory Show opened in New York on February 17, 1913, the general surge of interest in the arts "came to a head for us." About Duchamp's "Nude Descending a Staircase," Williams says, "I do remember how I laughed out loud when first I saw it, happily, with relief" (*Auto.*, 134). Williams did not know how to make use of the Frenchman's discoveries ("I confess I was slow to come up with any answers," *Auto.*, 136)—but that long-overdue laugh of relief is crucially important. The throat of beauty was slit before his eyes. It was shock therapy for the poet in a way that Flint's manifesto on Imagism in *Poetry* and Pound's "A Few Don'ts" could not be. After all, the first poem he wrote ("A black, black cloud") was an imagist poem; he didn't need to be told about it, he needed to be shaken and *shown*. It was courage, not instruction, that he lacked.

Once he began to feel that he was not alone, that he was not the only heretic to despise the work of Joyce Kilmer and other honored members of the Poetry Society of America, his poetry began to change rapidly. By the end of 1913, he had made contact with Alfred Kreymborg, who was living at the time in Grantwood, New Jersey, with Man Ray, plotting magazines.

The era of the little magazine has been too well documented, by thesis and by memoir, to require further description here. For historical convenience, the birth of Harriet Monroe's *Poetry* is generally conceded to mark the beginning of this remarkable period. In *Poetry* (June 1913) Williams made his American magazine debut with five poems, the last of which compares the American literary scene to a cemetery. He says the scene evokes a feeling of death:

> That unpleasant sense which one has when one smothers,
> Unhappy to leave so much behind merely to resemble
>   others
> It's good no doubt to lie socially well ordered when one
>   has so long to lie,
> But for myself somehow this does not satisfy.[5]

Apparently rejecting preestablished verse patterns to which he himself often felt enslaved, he merely expresses dissatisfaction without proposing alternatives. In 1914, Pound helped him get his work into London's *Egoist* magazine. One of the most interesting of Williams' poems to appear there that year is "La Flor," a panegyric on Pound, written in lanky, Whitmanesque lines. In it, Williams dismisses certain poets:

> our industrious versifiers—
> Those who bring their ingenious tapestries to such soft
>   perfection,
> Borrowing majesty . . .[6]

Pound liked the poem, not just because of the compliment to himself, but because "Your vocabulary is right." He adds, "Your syntax still strays from the simple order of natural speech." Toward the end of his letter, he makes an uncharacteristic admission: "You may get something slogging away by yourself that you would miss in The Vortex—and that we miss."[7]

Another poem Williams published that year in the *Egoist* is called "Aux Imagistes":

> I think I have never been so exalted
> As I am now by you,
> O frostbitten blossoms,
> That are unfolding your wings
> From out the envious black branches
>
> Bloom quickly and make much of the sunshine.
> The twigs conspire against you!
> Hear them!
> They hold you from behind!
> You shall not take wing
> Except wing by wing, brokenly.
> And yet——
> Even they
> Shall not endure for ever.[8]

Despite some fine visualizations, Williams still seems to confuse image with symbol, just as Pound, in the "Metro" poem, confuses image with metaphor. The fact is, Imagism never was defined in a way that could be applied to its major practitioners. Nor is it particularly important that it should be. "Aux Imagistes" is Williams' salute across the water to those who were fighting a battle similar to but not the same as his own. Considering Pound's emphasis on scholarship, and particularly on Chinese scholarship, it is little wonder that his sector of the imagist propaganda war was co-opted so easily by Amy Lowell and her "Chinoiseries," poems which display only the shakiest understanding of the Chinese poetry which they purport to imitate. Bloom quickly, Imagists, says Williams, and make the most of the publicity; it can't last.

By now, Williams was beginning to find his own people— Alfred Kreymborg, Mina Loy, Marianne Moore, Wallace Stevens, and others—but "no one knew consistently enough to formulate a 'movement.' " As he wrote later: "We were restless and constrained, closely allied with the painters. Impressionism, dadaism, surrealism applied to both painting and the poem. . . . We had followed Pound's instructions, his famous 'Don'ts,' eschewing inversions of phrase. . . . Literary allusions, save in very attenuated form, were unknown to us. Few had the necessary reading. . . . To my mind the thing that gave us most a semblance of a cause was not imagism, as some thought, but the line: the poetic line and our hopes for its recovery from stodginess." The ultimate aim, in his view, was to force the words of their poems "into approximation with experience rather than reading" (*Auto.*, 148).

The first major achievement of this aim occurs in "The Wanderer," Williams' long poem written just after *The Tempers*, and published by Pound in the *Egoist* in 1914. "Literary Innocence Regained," the poem might better have been titled. To continue identifying genres for Williams' poetry after the appearance of "The Wanderer" is to ignore that poem's meaning. The immersion in experience represented by the poet's baptism in the filthy Passaic River was paradoxically a commitment to a kind of literary innocence. Who can deny the literary innocence of a man who says, in a newspaper interview decades later, that a writer "can't shade the truth.

When he does he's a shyster if there ever was one. God! Imagine writing something knowing it's not true."[9]

From this time forward, the battle lines were drawn in the "persistent struggle between the raw new and the graciousness of an imposed cultural design" (*SE*, 138). All sonnets mean the same thing. The meaning is in the configuration. Therefore, the sonnet, or *any other* predetermined form, is inappropriate as a vehicle for capturing (without smothering) the "raw new." For Williams, reality is more than sonnet-fodder, it has its own shapes, its own "agony of line like the back-side or a lovely thigh," as Kay Boyle put it (*SL*, 129); and the poetic line had better try to follow it.

Even within "The Wanderer," the narrator "strongly guessed all that I must put from me / To come through ready for the high courses." The thought that he must put from him almost everything he had learned and grown to love brought with it a wave of despair:

> I heavy of heart
> For I knew the novitiate was ended
> The ecstasy was over, the life begun.   [*CEP*, 10]

Fortunately, there were friends ready to help make that life bearable and to nurture its growth. Kreymborg was starting a magazine called *Others*, "the magazine which . . . saved my life as a writer," as Williams succinctly describes it (*Auto.*, 135). Having made his internal commitments, aesthetic and existential, Williams finally began to let himself go in his writing. Kreymborg's description of Williams at this time is wonderfully evocative:

Shy though Bill was in person, blank paper let loose anything he felt about everything, and he frankly and fearlessly undressed himself down to the ground. . . . Among the first contributors to Others, no person gave as much of himself as Bill Williams. Regardless of the many patients who required his attention in and around the gray town of Rutherford, the medico often pointed the blunt nose of his Ford toward Grantwood or wrote incisive letters to Krimmie [Kreymborg] and aided him critically in the onerous task of choosing and rejecting manuscripts. . . . His letters, as outspoken as his poems, attacked and applauded Krimmie in the same paragraph, and for the sake of clarity many a goddam was thrown at the editor—and thrown back in rebuttal. At the close of such an exchange of civilities, Bill would laugh, turn on himself—another favorite pastime—and subject the patient to a surgical operation in which no phase of the raw spirit was spared. Groans would issue from the defenceless ego, and then someone had to treat him like the adolescent he was at such times. Shyness, bravado, imagination, scientific accuracy, childishness were constantly at war in [him].[10]

From this description, one senses in Williams a great reservoir of creative energy—amounting almost to violence—finding at last a channel for release. One also senses a great vulnerability, and a new willingness to be *seen* as vulnerable by other people.[11]

The first issue of the magazine appeared in July 1915, and it contained, as seems to be customary in new magazines, work by the editor, and even work *about* the editor (Orrick Johns' parodies of Kreymborg's *Mushrooms*). Were it not for some fine surrealistic lines by Mina Loy ("We might have given birth to a butterfly / With the daily news / Printed in blood on its wings"), the debut of *Others* would have to be called undistinguished. But the second issue (August 1915), containing four tight lyrics by Williams and Stevens' "Peter Quince at the Clavier," established *Others* as the most important avant-garde magazine in America. The third issue confirmed this impression by opening with T. S. Eliot's "Portrait of a Lady."

From the outset, *Others* had been greeted with hilarity in the established press, but after a few issues, praise began to be mingled with the general derision. *Life* magazine suggested to its readers that "it is worth the price of a Wednesday matinee to find out [about *Others*]. By the way, the new poetry *is* revolutionary. It is the expression of a democracy of feeling rebelling against an aristocracy of form."[12] That description accurately conveys the general tone of the magazine, and it certainly conveys the tone of the new work Williams was publishing there.

The first poem of Williams' to appear in *Others*, called "Pastoral," gives a good idea of what he is up to:

> The little sparrows
> Hop ingenuously
> About the pavement
> Quarreling
> With sharp voices
> Over those things
> That interest them.
> But we who are wiser
> Shut ourselves in
> On either hand
> And no one knows
> Whether we think good
> Or evil.
>
>   Then again,
> The old man who goes about
> Gathering dog-lime
> Walks in the gutter
> Without looking up
> And his tread
> Is more majestic than
> That of the Episcopal minister
> Approaching the pulpit

Of a Sunday.
These things
Astonish me beyond words.

When Williams reprinted the poem in *CEP* (124), he made several minor changes: "Then again" is changed to "Meanwhile," capital letters are dropped from the beginning of each line, and the penultimate line, "These things," is indented, indicating a break or pause, but not so great a one as that which separates the two stanzas. The minuteness of these differences and their subtle importance suggest the care with which Williams constructed his so-called free verse. The shift from "Then again" to "Meanwhile," for instance, softens the relationship of the first to the second stanza from an opposition to a simultaneity.

To define the charm of "Pastoral" is not easy. Linda Wagner's brief discussion of the poem notes that Williams is moving "into the human world through reference to nature. Here 'ingenuous' sparrows are superior to men because they reveal their emotions; similarly, man close to nature ('gathering doglime') is superior to man living amid the abstractions of civilization (the Episcopal minister). Innate majesty and dignity are one with the natural in the poet's sight."[13] Her remarks may be just; if so, they point up the inadequacy, not to say silliness, of paraphrase. Indeed, from such a summary, one cannot imagine what it was that astonished the poet "beyond words."

Breslin accuses Williams of sermonizing in this poem, and perhaps for some readers the last two lines and the phrase "more majestic" detract from the delight which the poem starts to arouse. For other readers, these moral impingements are essential trade-marks of Williams' style. "Intensity (i.e. simplicity)" is one of Pound's most profound literary equa-

tions.[14] Williams had already "put from him" a great deal
since writing "The Wanderer"; but the present poem shows
that he hadn't yet learned that to *say* he is astonished, at least
in so blatant a manner, drains away the reader's astonishment.
A purist might in fact strike a red pencil through the whole
last stanza.

Surprisingly, a comparison of manuscripts reveals that the
first stanza was probably written after the second (see "Pastoral 1" in Appendix A). Williams apparently started out with
the heavy moral comparison between the old man and the
minister, then halfway through yielded to the simple image of
sparrows hopping about on the pavement. The fact that the
poem breaks apart so easily in the middle suggests that Williams has unknowingly written two different poems. The tag
lines, "These things / Astonish me beyond words," show not
only his distrust of the adequacy of "mere" imagery but also
his secret doubts about the structural integrity of the poem.
Imagism as a movement waned, he said later, because it failed
to uncover a "structural necessity." An image is not a poem.
He sensed this, but he had yet to learn that an image with a
moral attached is not a poem either.

His method in these transitional poems, most of which he
published in *Al Que Quiere!*, is often to start with an image,
then either moralize it, or in some way assert that it is important. In another poem called "Pastoral," he makes the assertion backhandedly, and with greater aesthetic success, ending with

> No one
> will believe this
> of vast import to the nation.   [*CEP*, 121]

Another poem, "Apology," begins, "Why do I write today?"
surely a question one should ask *before* one writes. And one

still encounters an occasional Phoebus or other classical reference, thrown in for no apparent reason.

"The Shadow" (*CEP*, 120) is a different case. The poem
may strike one at first as being incredibly escapist, considering the climate of world events in the spring of 1914, when
it was written. After all, Williams is by now strenuous in his
assertions of the need for "contact" with the actualities of the
world. But *is* the poem escapist? Is a seed escapist for hiding
in the earth?

The following is an early version of "The Shadow," found
in a letter to Viola Jordan (née Baxter), dated April 29, 1914
(YALC):

> Soft as the bed in the earth
> > where a stone has lain;
> So soft, so smooth and so dark—
> Spring closes me in with her arms and her hands.
> Rich as the smell of new earth
> > loosed from a stone
> That has lain breathing the damp through its pores
> Spring closes me in with her blossomy hair, —
> > brings dark to my eyes.

There is a strong similarity between this poem and the unpublished "Self-Portrait 1" (the first lyric in Appendix A),
which begins, "You lie packed, / Dark. . . ." It is also closely
similar in theme to "Spring Song," written perhaps a few
months later, which begins and ends as follows:

> Having died
> one is at great advantage
> over his fellows—
> one can pretend,
>
> . . . . .
> I would merely lie
> hand in hand in the dirt with you.   [*CEP*, 119]

James Guimond argues that in "The Wanderer," and presumably in these other poems written shortly afterward, Williams is thinking of the myth of Demeter and Persephone. I
will not contend that he was ignorant of the myth, particularly so soon before the writing of *Kora in Hell;* but perhaps
he would have written very similar poetry even if he hadn't
known the myth. Bob Dylan warns that if you're not "busy
being born" you're busy dying. Williams was busy doing
both, at profound levels of the psyche. The myth is a coinci-
dence, a convenient handle, unimportant. But Guimond is
right about the relation of archetype to poetic technique:

New beings and instinctual drives are extremely inarticulate. Dis-
covering their presences and values is only the first of the artist's
responsibilities. He must still fulfill and communicate them by
enabling them to realize their true, unique forms . . . and therefore it is the artist who is a pioneer—who uses primitive, autoch-
thonous materials—that needs most to be a good craftsman.[15]

The early version of "The Shadow" can tell us something
about Williams' poetic craftsmanship at this time. First, there
are two changes in the vocabulary of the poem between the
early and the final versions. Instead of "so soft, so smooth and
so dark," the third line is corrected to read, "so soft, so smooth
and so cool." One reason for the change seems to be that
Williams wants to save "dark" for the last line ("brings dark
to my eyes"), and not waste its effectiveness by using it near
the beginning, where another word will do. Secondly, the
word "cool" picks up the sensual sound of "smooth" in a way
that "dark" does not. The other change in vocabulary seems
at first unfortunate. The word "loosed" in the lines "Rich as
the smell of new earth / loosed from a stone" functions ki-
netically, giving one the sense of a stone's being lifted from
its place, the earth falling away from it, releasing the rich

smell. This excitement is lost—consciously sacrificed—in the final version:

> Rich as the smell
> of new earth on a stone.

The word "on" conveys nothing, no motion whatsoever. But that is the point. The "I" of the poem is passive in his dark bed; he is like a stone, a corpse. Only personified spring—Primavera—is active, and her activity is to close him in, bury him. The word "loosed," with its opposite connotations, has to go.

Then there is the matter of form. Instead of one nine-line stanza, with the shorter lines indented to suggest interweaving, the final version is more formal, two stanzas, five and seven lines respectively, all lines approximately the same length:

> Soft as the bed in the earth
> where a stone has lain—
> so soft, so smooth and so cool
> Spring closes me in
> with her arms and her hands.
>
> Rich as the smell
> of new earth on a stone
> that has lain breathing
> the damp through its pores—
> Spring closes me in
> with her blossomy hair
> brings dark to my eyes.

Again, something valuable has been sacrificed, a sense of flow is traded for a feeling of solidity and perhaps propriety. One senses, though, that the change in shape has little to do with the tone or meaning of this particular poem but reflects a new general policy, adopted in the hope of firming up the structure of his too free verse. Describing his work in the pe-

riod immediately preceding the publication of *Al Que Quiere!*,
Williams writes, "The stanzas are short; I was searching for
some formal arrangement of the lines, perhaps a stanzaic form.
I have always had something to say and the sheer sense of
what is spoken seemed to me all important, yet I knew the
poem must have shape. From this time on you can see the
struggle to get a form without deforming the language"
(*IWWP*, 22–23).

With these formal questions still unresolved, psychological
and practical questions became pressing—what, for instance,
to do with a growing sheaf of eccentric, commercially un-
acceptable verse? As early as July 1916, a year after "The
Shadow" was published in *Poetry*, Williams entered into an
excited correspondence with Edmund Brown, owner and op-
erator of the Four Seas Publishing Company in Boston, about
bringing out a book of poems to be called *Pagan Promises*
(later the title was changed to *Al Que Quiere!*, and a heavily
ironic subtitle, *The Pleasures of Democracy*, was dropped).
No biographer could reveal Williams' state of mind at this
period better than Williams himself does in these letters.[16]
Here is a sampling:

[*July 18, 1916*]
The matter is that I must have a book out soon or I shall
destroy nearly all I have written. I seem only to be able to tolerate 50 or 60 of my things at a time. As I write the new, the old
dies off at the other end of the string.

[*July 19, 1916*]
"Fifty dollars! Fifty dollars! Do you know what that is, fifty
dollars? It's a weight would drag a man to the ground." That's a
translation from a Spanish peasant's conversation.

[*November 7, 1916*]
We can't sell "Others," neither can we give it away. It will

always exist, in whatever form it may be, even if only as a threat to conventional mediocrity.

It will continue to hold an avenue open for those expressions that are blocked elsewhere.

The name "Others" is alive today but the immediate need of the magazine is not as urgent as was the need a year and a half ago.

We will consider it a great courtesy if you will complete our unexpired subscriptions with your Journal. . . . [*Others* continued sporadically, however, until 1919.]

[*February 20, 1917*]
[*He is worried about a clause in the contract concerning "prosecution for scandalous content."*]

[*May 28, 1917*]
You don't like my pencil sketch of my own phiz do you? Look it up, if you have it there. I like it. Put it in center of cover. . . . It's a strange book to me. Doesn't seem as if I had written it at all. There are several unpleasant things in it I really would like to see cut out of it but—I can't bring myself to do it. One thing I would like you to do: delete "Gloriamini Verae etc." and put in its place "Ballet" the MSS of which I sent you in a recent letter. PLEASE DO NOT FAIL ME IN THIS!

[*September 29, 1917*]
No, I refuse to have the silhouette of my bean on any book published in Beantown. [Brown had lost the original sketch.] If the enclosed seems inappropriate to you simply put a circle about an inch in diameter in the center of the page so:

If you like my little pet monstrosity as inclosed [*sic.*], reduce it
to the size desired and slap it on.

                                        [*February 12, 1918*]
I have seen no reviews. The silence is complete, makes me happy
as I'd be in a wood, a true forest, some August noon. Great!

                                          [*March 11, 1918*]
My friends seem impressed but puzzled.

The "pet monstrosity" described in the letter of September
29th was probably the design which Brown ultimately used
for the cover of the book. It is copied from the markings on
a pebble, and looks like this:

Williams describes the figure this way: "To me the design
looked like a dancer, and the effect of the dancer was very
important—a natural, completely individual pattern. The artist made the outline around the design too geometrical; it
should have been irregular, as the pebble was" (*IWWP*, 18).
Although the design is intrinsically interesting, its significance
is unavailable to the reader without an explanation. Williams
did not bother explaining it until forty years after the book
appeared. The cryptic insignia is a sign saying "Private." It
suggests a defensive as well as an aggressive posture. The *Au-*

tobiography describes the "bitter pleasure" young Williams expected to derive from writing, "bitter because I instinctively knew no one much would listen. So what? . . . to hell with them all" (48–49). By trying to make his own poems into "natural, completely individual patterns," as idiosyncratic as the design on a common pebble, Williams assumed, with a tinge of anger, that he would never find a wide audience— for most people like what they can recognize, they "know what they like." The untranslated Spanish title, and the epigraph, also in Spanish, by the Guatemalan poet Rafael Arévalo Martínez,[17] are further indications of Williams' disregard for the common reader. In this snobbery he is ironically like Ezra Pound, whose posturings as an aloof and scholarly genius Williams could never stomach. Even the publisher Edmund Brown developed some of the same symptoms, and in an aggressively defensive jacket blurb warned the "gentle reader" that the book was "brutally powerful and scornfully crude," adding, "fortunately, neither the author nor the publisher care much whether you like it or not."

Although Williams insisted that his third book be as "secret" as the two which preceded it, drawing, for instance, on the complex of associations connected with his Spanish heritage, *Al Que Quiere!* is his most outward-directed book to date. He has by now firmly adopted the soil under his feet, and he expostulates to his fellow townspeople like a genuine incarnation of Whitman:

> Therefore listen!
> For you will not soon have another singer.   [*CEP*, 126]

There is also a much greater naturalness of language and particularity of physical description than formerly. "Sympa-

thetic Portrait of a Child," a poem about a murderer's little
daughter, makes an interesting contrast to the poem "Hic
Jacet," in *The Tempers*, about the "coroner's merry little
children." In both, Williams' approach is conceptual: to make
a statement about character traits and the extent to which they
are transmitted from parent to child. Both poems are gleefully
perverse in their conclusions: the humorless coroner (descen-
dant of the Puritan) has merry children (no character transmission); the murderer (spiritual Indian, outlaw) has an apparently innocent little daughter who flirts with the poet in a
way that is anything but innocent, and whose smile is a
"knife" (suggesting that there is a transmission of character).
But whereas in the earlier lyric the concept is the central element, in "Sympathetic Portrait" the idea gives way immediately to an excitingly exact observation of a child's behavior,
laid down on the page in irregular "free verse" lines whose
subtle enjambments heighten the enjoyed tension:

> The murderer's little daughter
> who is barely ten years old
> jerks her shoulders
> right and left
> so as to catch a glimpse of me
> without turning round.
>
> Her skinny little arms
> wrap themselves
> this way then that
> reversely about her body!
> Nervously
> she crushes her straw hat
> about her eyes
> and tilts her head
> to deepen the shadow—
> smiling excitedly!

As best she can
she hides herself
in the full sunlight
her cordy legs writhing
beneath the little flowered dress
that leaves them bare
from mid-thigh to ankle—

Why has she chosen me
for the knife
that darts along her smile?   [*CEP*, 155]

The final three lines, structurally equivalent to other tags Williams was using at this time, such as "These things / astonish me beyond words," are weaker than the rest of the poem because they rest so heavily upon a metaphor ("the knife"); but they help as much as they harm the poem—"knife" after all is a strikingly apt metaphor—and one cannot wish them canceled. Anyway, the poem has already been so successful in the *presentation* of its subject that Williams' conclusion (with its "idea") cannot be offensive. His perfect evocation of "cordy legs" and twisting shoulders has earned him the right to draw whatever conclusion he wishes. In comparison, the coroner's children seem pale and theoretical; one distrusts the poem in which they appear.

Many factors contribute to the sense of greater authenticity that the poems in *Al Que Quiere!* convey; among them one would have to list Williams' continuing interest in play writing. In fact, one poem, "Portrait of a Woman in Bed," appears with only minor changes in *Others* (April/May, 1919) as part of the dialogue of a verse play, *The Comic Life of Elia Brobitza*. An interesting critical exercise would be to try to determine which came first, whether Williams saw the poem in the play or the play in the poem. One suspects the latter, but

the contention would be hard to prove. In the play, the lines
are longer than they are in the poem, and the line breaks are
often more radical. Does this indicate later composition? If so,
why was not the poem changed in conformity with the new
pattern before being reprinted? The following excerpts will
perhaps lead the reader to his own conclusions. First, from the
poem:

> I won't work
> and I've got no cash.
> What are you going to do
> about it?
> —and no jewelry
> (the crazy fools)
>
> But I've my two eyes
> and a smooth face
> and here's this! Look!
> it's high!
>
> There's brains and blood
> in there—
> my name's Robitza!
> Corsets
> can go to the devil—
> and drawers along with them—
> What do I care!   [*CEP*, 150]

Then, from the play:

> *She*
> I won't work and I got no cash;
> what are you going to do about
> it?—and no jewelry—the crazy
> fools! But I've my two eyes and a
> smooth face and here's this, look!
> it's high! There's brains and blood in there!
> my name's Brobitza!

(Pause. She looks up slyly as the officer makes a move as if to draw back the covers)

Corsets can go to the devil and
drawers along with them! What do I care.

(She laughs coarsely.)

There is a good deal of strong writing in *Al Que Quiere!*, as the lines just quoted suggest, but the poems hardly seem "brutally powerful" today; after exposure to writers like Ginsberg, Burroughs, and Gênet, we need to exercise some historical imagination to understand Brown's statement or Williams' fears about being prosecuted for scandalous content. But it is our failure, and a serious one, if we cannot be shocked with the violence of lines like these:

I saw a child with daisies
for weaving into the hair
tear the stems
with her teeth!   [*CEP*, 122]

What is most striking about all the poems in the book is their energy. Like Antaeus, whose strength suddenly redoubled when he touched the ground, Williams found vast resources of energy in himself as soon as he abandoned the abstractions of his earlier work and "confined" himself to mundane subjects, a woman in bed, buds on a tree, a glass filled with parsley beside the kitchen sink.

One's reaction to the poems in *Al Que Quiere!* is likely to be the same as Williams' reaction to the Armory Show of 1913: a laugh of relief. One is relieved not only by the greater naturalness of the language but by the lifting of restrictions on subject matter as well. Why, a poem can be made about *anything*, one seems to hear Williams saying in these pages,

with quiet amazement in his voice. Even, perhaps, about one's
own nose:

> Oh strong-ridged and deeply hollowed
> nose of mine! what will you not be smelling?
> What tactless asses we are, you and I boney nose
> always indiscriminate, always unashamed,
> and now it is the souring flowers of the bedraggled
> poplars: a festering pulp on the wet earth
> beneath them. With what deep thirst
> we quicken our desires
> to that rank odor of a passing springtime!
> Can you not be decent? Can you not reserve your ardors
> for something less unlovely? What girl will care
> for us, do you think, if we continue in these ways?
> Must you taste everything? Must you know everything?
> Must you have a part in everything?   [*CEP*, 153]

Williams's realization that a poem can be made of anything
at all could have originated in his reading of Whitman as
easily as in his experience of the Armory Show. This poem
on the poet's nose, for instance, is reminiscent of several passages in "Song of Myself" in which Whitman stands aside
from his own body and examines it with curious detachment.
"What I am," he says,

> Stands amused, complacent, compassionating, idle, unitary,
> Looks down, is erect, bends an arm on an impalpable cer-
>   tain rest,
> Looks with its sidecurved head curious what will come
>   next.[18]

In Williams' nose poem, the delight is uncompromised by
symbols, stilted diction, or assertions of the subject's significance. It is a better poem than "Promenade," for example, in
which the poet addresses his own mind ("Well, mind, here

we have"). The mind has its dualities, to be sure, but no one can address his own mind; the poem is therefore based on a false premise, and the reader is embarrassed for the poet. Not so in the case of the nose, a physical thing separable from the consciousness, which one does in fact carry around with one, almost like a companion. Given this basic plausibility, the numerous delights of the poem are free to develop. For some reason, noses, when described in isolation from other bodily features, can never be treated seriously in literature (sad fact!). Like bald heads, they are always a subject for comedy, usually ribald comedy. More than any other protuberance, the nose excites man's risibility. Thus, the opening apostrophe ("Oh strong-ridged . . ."), leaping an enjambment and landing flatly on the "nose" at the beginning of line two, sets the bathetic tone for the whole piece. The sorrowful scolding by the nose's accomplice in indecency is couched in language just slightly elevated from the actual language of exasperation. "What will you not be smelling" is not quite colloquial, but not stilted either; it balances on a thin comedic line that suggests an older, wearier, more educated companion to the boorish nose. The speaker's incessant rhetorical questions fill in further his character sketch.

But informing and inspiring the playfulness of the poem is the truth that underlies it. The "rank odor" of a "festering pulp on the wet earth"—an implicitly sexual description, as highly charged as any in the book—represents the actual, the experiential, the physical, for which the poet has been starved for so long. Yet Williams has written: "In theme, the poems of *Al Que Quiere!* reflect things around me. I was finding out about life. Rather late, I imagine. This was a quiet period, a pre-sex period, although I was married" (*IWWP*, 23). This

sentence is so astonishing, in view of the sexual overtones in
many of the poems, that one feels it must somehow be true.
But it is not true. Williams must have been thinking of the
shy "Love Song" to Flossie, forgetting other poems, such as
the cryptic "Virtue," in which we find

> whirlpools . . .
> . . . . .
> funneling down upon
> the steaming phallus-head
> of the mad sun himself . . . [*CEP*, 152]

And he was forgetting the delightful "Canthara," which com-
bines (not for the first time in the book) the motifs of dance
and sexuality:

> The old black-man showed me
> how he had been shocked
> in his youth
> by six women, dancing
> a set-dance, stark naked below
> the skirts raised round
> their breasts:
>   bellies flung forward
> knees flying!
>   —While
> his gestures, against the
> tiled wall of the dingy bath-room,
> swished with ecstasy to
> the familiar music of
>   his old emotion.   [*CEP*, 143]

Williams' early thirties may have been a quiet period (that
too is unlikely), but it was certainly not a "pre-sex" period,
unless Williams attaches to that term some private meaning
that can no longer be deciphered. Sex is the round dance to
which he is beginning to learn the steps. In "Danse Russe," a

companion piece to "Canthara," we are offered the spectacle
of the poet dancing naked,

>   grotesquely
> before my mirror
> waving my shirt round my head
> and singing.   [*CEP*, 148]

One is reminded of his remarks about the pebble: "To me the
design looked like a dancer, and the effect of the dancer was
very important—a natural, completely individual pattern"
(*IWWP*, 18). The concern with dance stays with him all his
life, from a 1908 letter to Ed about Isadora Duncan to the last
lines of *Paterson:*

> We know nothing and can know nothing
>   but
> the dance, to dance to a measure
> contrapuntally,
>   Satyrically, the tragic foot. [*Pat.*, 278]

In "Danse Russe," Williams is already the satyr dancing to
the pagan *tragos*, the goat-song of Pan. Sex, music, dance are
already inextricably connected for him, and will remain so.
And they are all convertible terms for poetry. Not "beautiful" poetry anymore—the poet dances "grotesquely," and in
the first poem in the book ("Sub Terra") is looking for "grotesque fellows . . . to make up my band" (see also the last
poem in Appendix A, titled "Grotesque"). But in sacrificing
obvious beauties, such as those attending the artful execution
of a sonnet, Williams has opened his writing up to the actual
world and discovered the world to be available for poetic
uses. He still has not learned how to exploit this discovery
fully, but despite the formal problems, his allegiance is now
firmly pledged to the individual iridescences of reality, however grotesque, tawdry, or even beautiful they may appear.

CHAPTER THREE

Kora in Hell: Improvisations

One year after *Al Que Quiere!* appeared, Williams wrote to Brown:

> I want to have published this spring a volume of poems, so to speak — short pieces, paragraph length which I have named Improvisations. It will be a full sized book.
> I offer you first refusal remembering your services to me in the past.
> It is important to me that the book be brought out this spring. If you are interested ask to see MSS., if not, please let me know promptly.[1] [YALC]

The "poems, so to speak" were later to be given the title *Kora in Hell: Improvisations* and published, in a shorter form than originally intended, in September 1920. The book is even more secret and personal than the three previous ones: "It reveals myself to me and perhaps that is why I have kept it to myself" (*IWWP*, 26). In the last decade, though, critics and scholars have discovered the book and have offered numerous interpretations, some quite intelligent, but almost all of them too general. Quotations have been culled from the Prologue and from the Improvisations themselves to show what Williams "means" or what the book "represents" in relation to his artistic development, but rarely to show how the writing *works.*

Two statements by Williams will indicate his general approach. The first is from the notorious Prologue: "Thus, seeing the thing itself without forethought or afterthought but with great intensity of perception, my mother loses her bearings or associates with some disreputable person or translates a dark mood. She is a creature of great imagination" (*Imag.*, 8). The second is from a later essay, called "A Beginning on the Short Story (Notes)":

> How does one take to the imagination? One may recognize its approach in that its first signs are like those of falling asleep. . . . At first all the images, one or many which fill the mind, are fixed. . . . We look at the ceiling and review the fixities of the day, the month, the year, the lifetime. Then it begins: that happy time when the image becomes broken or begins to break up, becomes a little fluid. The rigidities yield—like ice in March, the magic month. . . . Write down anything that seems pertinent to the subject or to no subject. Get into the fluid state, for unless you do, all you will say will be valueless.   [*SE*, 307]

Losing one's bearings, falling asleep—these acts do not imply any vagueness of perception. Nothing is more specific or more intensely convincing than a dream; only our later memory of it tends to be vague. Thus Williams, the poet of concrete particulars, can write that "The poem is a dream" (*SE*, 281). The difference between the particulars of a dream and those of our daily consciousness is that the former have been released from their "malignant rigidities" and set free to recombine in startling ways—in juxtapositions similar to those in Cubist paintings.[2] In fact the book is set up in patterns of jarring stylistic juxtaposition: first a prose-poem, then a commentary, printed in italics. The following example (XII, 2) illustrates many of the book's qualities and techniques:

> The trick is never to touch the world anywhere. Leave your-self at the door, walk in, admire the pictures, talk a few words with the master of the house, question his wife a little, rejoin yourself at the door—and go off arm in arm listening to last week's symphony played by angel hornsmen from the benches of a turned cloud. Or if dogs rub too close and the poor are too much out   let your friend answer them.

The poet being sad at the misery he has beheld that morning and seeing several laughing fellows approaching puts himself in their way in order to hear what they are saying. Gathering from their remarks that it is of some sharp business by which they have all made an inordinate profit, he allows his thoughts to play back upon the current of his own life. And imagining himself to be two persons he eases his mind by putting his burdens upon one while the other takes what pleasure there is before him.

Something to grow used to; a stone too big for ox haul, too near for blasting. Take the road round it or—scrape away, scrape away: a mountain's buried in the dirt! Marry a gopher to help you! Drive her in! Go yourself down along the lit pastures. Down, down. The whole family take shovels, babies and all! Down, down! Here's Tenochtitlán! here's a strange Darien where worms are princes. [*Imag.*, 53]

Occasionally, as here, there are three or even four sections, but usually there are only two sections in any given sequence in *Kora* (and several sequences to a "chapter"). When there are two, the second section functions as a distorting mirror to the first. As Williams says of mirrors later in the book (XXV, 1), "Nothing of a mechanical nature could be more conducive to that elasticity of the attention which frees the mind for the enjoyment of its special prerogatives" (*Imag.*, 78). The careful reader should be able to tell that this statement appears in one of the italicized sections of *Kora*. The vocabulary in such sections more erudite, and the sentences are often draped with present participles, decorous clauses, and calm suspensions, suggesting not stuffiness but a detached observation that draws loose ends together into an imaginative synthesis.[3]

The first section of a given sequence (and the third, where there are three) is frequently choppy, full of imperatives, exclamations, and swift, minute observations, all delivered in the hyper-excited tones of one whose "self was being slaughtered" (*Auto.*, 158). Williams was deeply affected by the war, which was then raging, and by the demands upon his physical endurance made by the great influenza epidemic of 1918, when the phone would ring as often as sixty times a day. To add to the strain, it became evident that Williams' father was dying of cancer. The nonitalicized sections of each sequence in *Kora* were written at night, every night for a year. The writing apparently served as a needed release from the frantic demands of his personal and professional life. The circumstances of composition, then, may partly explain the martial Mahleresque tone of much of the book, a tone that the modern reader is more likely to tolerate than to enjoy.

Yet, as in the case of so many major American works, the flaws, the clumsinesses of *Kora* are inseparable from its virtues. *Al Que Quiere!* has wonderful flashes, but *Kora in Hell* is Williams' first work of genius. The constant exhausting routine and the continuous oppression of personal and global tragedy seem to have put Williams into that fluid state in which rigidities yield to the shaping imagination. He describes that state in the sequence quoted: *"He allows his thoughts to play back upon the current of his own life."* (The word "cur-

rent" here may be a conscious metaphor.) The next sentence
is equally revealing: "*And imagining himself to be two persons he eases his mind by putting his burdens upon one while
the other takes what pleasure there is before him.*" Williams
says several things at once in this sequence of *Kora*—indeed,
an "impressionistic view of the simultaneous" (*IWWP*, 29) is
his major artistic aim. It is therefore only a partial exegesis of
the sentence to say that Williams sees himself as two person-
alities: the sane, responsible doctor in a beleaguered community and a desperate poet flirting dangerously with madness.
Naturally, the latter person was the one who expressed himself first on paper after a day and night of house calls. All the
burdens were put on the doctor "while the other takes what
pleasure there is" in the sheet of paper before him. Later,
"without thought, or [without?] too much of it, I inter-
preted" (*Auto.*, 159), and the italicized sections, the doctor's
"objective" analyses, were the result.

It would be a mistake, however, to think that Williams'
chthonian self was kept strictly suppressed during the doctor's rounds. The keen appreciation of recalcitrant individuality and even perversity in Williams' semiautobiographical
fiction bears witness to its constant presence.[4] And the fact
that, in *Kora*, several short prose sections are bound together
in each sequence indicates that the different voices are meant
to be heard simultaneously, so far as that is possible in the
sequential realm of the printed word. (Some of Jackson Mac-
Low's recent experiments in tape overlays would appear to
have their origin in the method of *Kora*.) The *Autobiography*, too, is full of seditious asides unnoticed by the average
skimmer, in which this second voice can be heard alongside
the first. Describing the horrors of the influenza epidemic,
Williams notes, "I lost two young women in their early twen-

ties, the finest physical specimens you could imagine" (*Auto.*, 159–160). That is *Kora*—the insistence on noticing perfections where it is *outré*, even indecent, to notice them. "Have you not read my Improvisations?" Williams wrote to Kenneth Burke. "I have said there at least five hundred times that all things have their perfections and that perfection and perfection are equal. It is my sole contribution to the world of my own senses. Drink" (YALC).[5]

The two voices in *Kora*, then, are not to be distinguished by their objectivity or lack of it—they both exhibit "great intensity of perception"—but by their tone and diction. The "chthonian" voice throws up expostulations from the midst of experience; the other voice, speaking in Williams' "italic tone," mirrors that experience from within a calm Olympian realm of Imagination. Musically, the effect is a blend of percussion and strings; of fragment and of flow. It is not difficult to see in this alternation an analogy to the Whitman/Keats dichotomy that characterizes all of Williams' early work.

The fact that the three paragraphs in the sequence quoted are bound together into a numbered unit suggests not only a simultaneity but possibly an equality of meaning as well, as if the poet approached the second paragraph with the phrase "in other words" firmly in his mind. In the example before us, the relationships between paragraphs are fairly straightforward. The first paragraph posits a psychic split ("leave yourself at the door . . . rejoin yourself"); the second, seeming to explain the occasion for the writing of the first paragraph, describes the split in the particular terms of a poet's consciousness; the third shifts the category, but the sense of alternate modes of thinking and acting remains strong: "Take the road round it or—scrape away."

Difficulties remain, however. For Williams, the poet of

"contact," to write that "the trick is never to touch the world anywhere," is surely to signal the presence of an ironic, even comic, intention. The "angel hornsmen" playing "last week's symphony" confirm the suspicion and will remind the reader of the mermaids singing in the dreams of J. Alfred Prufrock, keeping reality at a pleasant distance ("if dogs rub too close"). Yet the second paragraph describes a similar psychic dissociation without any apparent satirical overtones. The outward man bears the burdens and overhears the deceits of the outward world, while the inner man takes pleasure, perhaps aesthetic pleasure, in the play of forces and actions about him *"without making the usual unhappy moral distinctions"* (IV, 3, *Imag.*, 38). A later Improvisation (XXV, 2) describes a human interaction as a *"beautiful design"* which elaborates itself *"much to the secret delight of the onlooker who is thus regaled by the spectacle of two exquisite and divergent natures playing one against the other"* (*Imag.*, 79–80).

The first two paragraphs, then, assuming they are not simply contradictory in meaning, contrast two kinds of detachment, one arising from a fear of reality, the other from a vast enjoyment of the interreactions between reality and imagination. The third paragraph, in which the terms of opposition are radically changed, reminds the reader of a statement in *A Novelette and Other Prose* about these early Improvisations: "Their excellence is, in major part, the shifting of category. It is the disjointing process" (*Imag.*, 285). In a sense, the third paragraph of the sequence is the obverse of the first. Instead of attempting to avoid touching the world, the voice of this paragraph advocates getting down and scraping in the dirt. No longer is there any detachment or "dissociation of sensibility." By the second sentence, the speaker has made his choice and follows out its consequences relentlessly, until the lost cities of the subconscious are found, a mountain un-earthed.

This sequence of the Improvisations leaves one feeling mild surprise that there is more symmetry and method here than one had expected to find. "Method, Method, what do you want from me?" exclaims Jules Laforgue in his *Moralités Légendaires*, "You know that I have eaten of the fruit of the subconscious."[6] Williams has, too; and yet there is a symmetry in these paragraphs that seems more than instinctive. The first and the third paragraphs, in exhortatory but carefully distinguished prose styles (the first advisory, the last exclamatory), offer their opposite philosophies. The first speaker argues for dissociation from the unsanitary physical world, and so from one's own physical being and natural human sympathies. The fictional vision the speaker evokes is that of an emotionally uncommitted visitor (a doctor?) in the house of a well-to-do married couple of some artistic pretensions. The scene evoked in the third paragraph has some of the atmospheric qualities of Melville's "I and My Chimney," or of Chapter 41 of *Moby Dick*, in which Ahab's soul is described in terms of the subbasement of the Cluny Monastery in Paris. The man/woman and man/world relationships described here are very different from those in paragraph one, without loss of the implicitly comedic tone: "The whole family take shovels, babies and all!" Between these extremes of Apollonian/Dionysian (or Puritan/Indian) consciousness, stands the calm middle paragraph in which the poet, in an explicitly realized street-scene out of Restoration comedy, expresses the *poetic* consciousness: one which sees both attitudes clearly and "takes what pleasure there is before him."

There seem, then, to be several viable readings of the sequence. No reading is entirely satisfactory; too little information is given the reader for a definitive interpretation. The withholding of external details makes for a passage that is "fraught with background," in Erich Auerbach's felicitous phrase. In this one way like *Genesis*, *Kora* projects voices from a psychic wilderness, crying "Here I am."[7] But the descriptive parallels, the controlled variations of diction, and the overall symmetry of the interlocked paragraphs suggest that *Kora* is more than the "automatic writing" Williams later implied that it was.

Williams meant something different by the term than, for example, Yeats did. He had a healthy respect for the subconscious as a source of energy and of imagery, and he wrote most of his best things swiftly while in that fluid dreamlike state he describes in a passage already quoted (*SE*, 307); but he never advocated complete submission to the subconscious. "Contact," inner and outer, does not in itself guarantee successful art, though it is a prerequisite. Control is necessary, but it must not be so tight that the flow stops. Williams never quite explains what he permitted himself in *Kora*, but the use of the term "permitted myself" (in the 1957 Prologue to the City Lights Edition) suggests a loosening rather than a tightening of the aesthetic reins in order to let through the forces he felt within him. In this sense, the writing of *Kora* was "automatic," and what he wrote he did not rewrite. He did, however, prune and rearrange.

The consciously worked symmetries such as those we have noticed are all local manifestations; no overall structure governs the book. If there is a general structural principle, it may be found through contemplation of the book's central metaphor, that of the dance. Unlike a march, a dance is not going anywhere. One may enter it at any point, leave and rejoin it. It is thus like Rilke's "song," which

> ist nicht Begehr,
> nicht Werbung um ein endlich noch Erreichtes;
> Gesang ist Dasein.[8]

Song is Being; not a striving toward later completion. *Kora* completes itself at each step along the way. As Schiller says of Homer, his goal is "already present in every point of his progress." The "chapters" of *Kora* are self-contained units, individual dances of the imagination, hovering over the page like wavering "heat over the end of a roadway that turns downhill" (*Imag.*, 47), or like dreams noted down upon awakening, whose primary connection with one another is the fact that the same mind dreamed them all.[9]

Impressionistic terms are unavoidable in attempting to describe a work as unique as this one. Not everyone agrees about its uniqueness. René Taupin, taking his cue from several letters Pound wrote to Williams, has uncovered numerous resemblances between *Kora* and Rimbaud's prose poems;[10] but the differences remain more profound than the similarities. Later, Pound was willing to concede at least that "I don't think [Williams] knew it was Rimbaud until after he finished his operation."[11] But this concession only changes the charge from willful plagiarism to literary stupidity. In fact, says Williams, "I was familiar with the typically French prose poem, its pace was not the same as my own compositions" (*Imag.*, 29). Sherman Paul's perceptive article on *Kora* in *The Shaken Realist* should help lay this question of Rimbaud's influence to rest. "It may be true . . . that Williams is very much like Rimbaud in gifts, intelligence, and spirit; that, like Rimbaud, he has a talent for irony, an eye for minute detail, a predilection for the commonplace and vulgar, even a profound concern for the dance of the imagination. But likeness is not necessarily influence, and in the most important element of

Taupin's comparison he is not like Rimbaud at all—in uniting
the power to contact things with the freest and most visionary
imagination. Williams is not a visionary poet."[12]
Many aspects of *Kora*—to take one example, the juxtaposition of paragraphs in order to create "an impressionistic view
of the simultaneous"—cannot be ascribed to any single influence or set of influences. The Cubists in painting, and writers
as different as Proust, Joyce, Stein, and Faulkner, were concerned with basically the same problem. "It has in a way been
the mission of the 20th century to destroy progressive history
and create a single time in which everything in the past and
possibly the future would be simultaneous," writes Donald
Sutherland in a book that does not even mention Williams.
"This time, which one might call legendary time, is the time
of the composition, or rather within the composition."[13] It is
just such a created continuous present that *Kora* carves out
for itself and occupies.

The artistic links connecting *Kora* with other major literary achievements of its time are useful to see, so long as one
does not lose awareness of the intense, even despairing, privacy
of the work. If Pound thought it was largely incoherent, what
could Williams expect from less acute readers? Possibly he
himself was not sure what he had done. The italicized sections
can be seen as an attempt to possess, or control, psychic and
literary elements that were not yet quite enough *out* of control. Williams was flirting with artistic chaos. "I thought of
myself as Springtime," he wrote (*IWWP*, 29), "and I felt I
was on my way to Hell (*but I didn't go very far*)" (italics
mine). In a letter about *Al Que Quiere!*, Wallace Stevens had
told Williams, "I think your tantrums not half mad enough"
(*Imag.*, 16). One can almost hear Williams, in *Kora*, answer-
ing, "Is *this* mad enough for you?" Finally, one sees two

struggles in *Kora:* the struggle to lose control, and the struggle to gain control. The need to submit, to allow, to "give up," as he put it in that 1934 letter to Marianne Moore (*SL*, 149), is followed immediately by the tinkering intellect's need to understand and to shape. It is in this conflict of needs that the most basic distinction between the italicized and nonitalicized sections is to be found.

In an article in *The Little Review*[14] laconically titled "More Swill," Williams speaks of "the eternal and until now slighted nature of the engagement between artist and critic. It is a dance! . . . That there is no transition between critic and artist I will maintain as well as I am able. A man may be one, then the other, but never one within the other." Might there not also be a dancelike relationship between the different voices in *Kora?* At any rate, the statement is suggestive and invites a lateral jump to Gaston Bachelard's discussion of the *animus* and *anima*. Attempting to characterize his own literary career, Bachelard situates it "under the contradictory signs, masculine and feminine, of the *concept* (m.) and the *image* (f.). Between the concept and the image, there is no synthesis. And there is no filiation either. . . . Whoever gives himself over to the concept with all his mind, over to the image with all his soul, knows perfectly well that concepts and images develop on two divergent planes of the spiritual life."[15]

It would be convenient to argue that the first paragraph of each sequence was written by the *anima*, and the italicized second paragraph by the *animus*. Quotations could be drawn from the correspondence with Viola Jordan to the effect that "men are not strong enough to 'bat air' with women[;] that forever proves to me that I am not a man; they, men, disgust me and if I must say it fill me with awe and admiration. I am too much a woman" (YALC).[16] That would be the *anima* speaking, as it does in section XIII, 1, of *Kora:* "Dig deeper *mon ami,* the rock maidens are running naked in the dark cellars" (*Imag.,* 54). The theory acquires some further plausibility when one considers that the italicized passages were all written as "explanations" of the improvisations they follow. Williams the poet is not, however, succeeded in the italicized paragraphs by Williams the critic, but by Williams the fiction writer. For example (in V, 3), after a paragraph in which the voice of poetic reverie hears the *"Fort sale!"* in the cry "For Sale!" the voice of narration takes over to provide a setting and perspective: *"A man whose brain is slowly curdling due to a syphilitic infection acquired in early life calls on a friend to go with him on a journey to the city. The friend out of compassion goes, and thinking of the condition of his unhappy companion, falls to pondering on the sights he sees as he is driven up one street and down another"* (*Imag.,* 40).

"Falls to pondering," "allows his thoughts to play back upon the current of his own life" (XII, 2), "loosen[s] their imaginations" (XXI, Coda): always the voice in italics refers backward, from a vantage point of impartial wakefulness, to the reveries and confused expostulations of the word dreamer deep in the "shells of speech" (*coquilles de parole,* in Bachelard's phrase).[17]

But whether or not the initial paragraph of a sequence was written "spontaneously," and the italicized explanation written with some artistic and/or critical calculation, it is evident that neither could serve as an example of the everyday American speech which Williams so strenuously advocated for use in poetry.

If one rejects Taupin's arguments concerning the central influence of the French prose poem, one is at a loss for a literary model for the nonitalicized passages. In fact, in tone and general strategy, the nearest literary precedent one can find for these emotion-wrenched paragraphs is Williams' own poem "Spring Strains," which Bram Dijkstra convincingly argues was modeled on the structural principles of Cubism. The influence of Cubism on *Kora* is, of course, as arguable as the influence of Rimbaud. Although both influences are present, their effect on the literary outcome was slight. In fact Williams wrote his hyperexcited paragraphs in a hyperexcited state of mind, letting one image or one idea lead immediately and without transition to the next—anticipating Olson's essay on "Projective Verse" by about thirty years.

What this suggests about Williams, however, is that his instinctive style, when in a certain frame of mind, bears little relation to natural American speech rhythms, whatever they may be. Williams once explained that he began using short lines in his poetry because he was in an excited, "breathless" state of mind when he wrote, and short lines best reflected and conducted this tension (*IWWP*, 15). A paragraph has no such conductor. Feeling the lack, he tried using spacing in ways that would affect the look and tempo of a passage. "*Most important!*" he wrote to Edmund Brown. "Set up the improvisations exactly as written. Do *not* add to or alter punctuation. Where there is a gap between two words – leave it" (YALC). We have seen an example of this method in the Improvisation (XII, 2) already quoted (". . . and the poor are too much out   let your friend answer them"). Despite these attempts at channeling his intense feelings and rhythms into adequate form, there is a sense of electrical overload to many of the paragraphs, as if Williams' prose could not handle the energy transfer. In certain of his prose writings an actual breakdown occurs and Williams is forced to leave a long sentence unfinished to go on to the next. Consider for example the following paragraph from the *Autobiography* (358):

All day long the doctor carries on this work, observing, weighing, comparing values of which neither he nor his patients may know the significance. He may be insensitive. But if in addition to actually being an accurate craftsman and a man of insight he has the added quality of—some distress of mind, a restless concern with the . . . If he is not satisfied with mere cures, if he lacks ambition, if he is content to . . . If there is no content in him and likely to be none; if in other words, without wishing to force it, since that would interfere with his lifelong observation, he allows himself to be called a name! What can one think of him?

In contemplating the failure of this paragraph, one must not be blind to its peculiar success. One of Williams' primary aims was to capture "the form of motion." This paragraph embodies the form of his own mind's motion while in "some distress." The poet is in the grip of his own meaning. At such points, the reader is likely to wonder whether Williams is extraordinarily clever, or whether he might be suffering from an incipient speech impediment which surfaces at moments of great excitement when no adequate form is immediately available for the embodiment of his violent feelings.

Admittedly, the nonitalicized paragraphs in *Kora* are more tightly compressed than is the prose of Williams' letters and critical essays; but like them they are composed of small verbal/emotional explosions and proceed by leaps over logical gaps. One might say that the rhythms of those passages are those of semiinarticulateness violently overcome. Speech was a tightrope for Williams which he found easier to cross at a run than at a walk. The speed of his nonitalicized paragraphs (frequently there is no time even for verbs) sometimes gets around reality fast enough to capture whole "*the imaginative qualities of the actual things being perceived,*" as he says in one commentary (XVIII, 3). The word "things" is somewhat misleading, however: "force" would be better. As he says in *Spring and All,* he needed "to practice skill in recording the force moving, then [perhaps through the italicized commentaries] to know it, in the largeness of its proportions" (*Imag.,* 120).

Kora in Hell offers one the unique opportunity to observe, in unblended form, Williams' two primary stylistic tendencies. The nonitalicized paragraphs are the impassioned expostulations of "Carlos," the inspired Spanish peasant. Their very bluntness is a kind of obscurity, deriving, one suspects, from the fools in Shakespeare's plays, from *El Romancero* and other folk literature, and especially from Williams' mother, "a creature of great imagination," who always sees "the thing itself without forethought or afterthought but with great intensity of perception" (*Imag.,* 8). But Williams was also the son of a cultured Englishman, and in the italicized paragraphs all his suppressed gentility surfaces in a pure form for the first and only time in his mature writings. Most often his prose is a mixture of the two elements: blunt, transitionless flashes of insight delivered with pugilistic force, but laced with strange inversions, which one recognizes as a deflected gentility left over from Williams' university days, when he was composing sonnets and writing to his brother "Bo" about "a judicious involvement of the meaning." Often the blend is not at all unpleasant, and it contributes to the uniqueness of Williams' prose voice. "If anything of moment results—so much the better," he begins *Spring and All.* "And so much the more likely will it be that no one will want to see it" (*Imag.,* 88). Strong and swift writing—but the visceral qualities are given dignity by the unconsciously highbrow diction: "anything of moment," "more likely will it be."

Literary precedents for Williams' "italic tone," then, are probably too numerous to identify. But there is one genre (if one may dignify it with that term) whose characteristics are strikingly similar to those of the italicized paragraphs in *Kora*. The following example, chosen at random, is a program note for a 1971 off-Broadway production (Osvaldo Dragón's *Historias para ser contadas*): "Listening to the advice of his wife who wants him to work constantly, and his dentist, who deceives him with expensive tests and medications to get his money, a man tries to neglect a toothache that grows by the minute, making life impossible for him." Here is another: "In a country at war, a woman acts as an informer against her husband, and then elaborates for her sons a melodramatic justification of her acts, based on a morbid sense of religion, morality, and devotion" (Fernando Arrabal's *Los dos verdugos*). The distanced narrative summary, decked in long participial phrases, exactly echoes the tone and pace of the italicized paragraphs of *Kora*. Consider again the sequence quoted near the beginning of the present chapter, or the following, from section XI, 2 (*Imag.*, 52):

> *Hilariously happy because of some obscure wine of the fancy which they have drunk four rollicking companions take delight in the thought that they have thus evaded the stringent laws of the county. Seeing the distant city bathed in moonlight and staring seriously at them they liken the moon to a cow and its light to milk.*

The question of whether or not Williams was aware that he was writing program notes for a play or a dance concert is finally unimportant. He intended a contrast of some sort, and a clarification of the action on a "higher" plane of thought.

Beyond that, one may speculate as one will, but one is in a realm where there are few certainties and few literary precedents to guide one. "The poetic act has no past," says Bachelard, who is not ignorant of the force of genre in literary history, but who finds a phenomenological approach—"that is to say, consideration of the *onset of the image* in [the reader's] consciousness"—to be ultimately more fruitful than pointing out parallels.[18] In the case of *Kora*, where the identification of precedents is conjectural at best, it is necessary to give in to Williams, to enter into a naive, present-tense state of mind in which each phrase becomes a "sudden salience," or one almost cannot read the book.

"A cracked window blind lets in Venus." The reader must stop and let that sentence happen to him, both ways. Then the next words:

Stars. The hand-lamp is too feeble to have its own way. The vanity of their neck stretching, trying to be large as a street-lamp sets him roaring to himself anew. And rubber gloves, the color of moist dates, the identical glisten and texture: means a balloon trip to Fez. [*Imag.*, 66]

One thing leads to another, as in dream. The rubber gloves hanging before the reader's eyes with all the actuality of an hallucination turn into dates, which come from Egypt, and suddenly the reader is in a Jules Verne balloon heading east. One is reminded of the method of Joyce's *Ulysses*, which began appearing in *The Little Review* in 1918, and which Williams followed with interest. Joyce's influence on Williams seems to have been a positive one; the Irishman challenged him, whereas Eliot threatened him. He felt for Joyce the kinship of a fellow innovator pushing at the boundaries of words.

Perhaps the ideal reader of this most difficult book of Williams' would be an intelligent eight-year-old child. To read it as a critic, noticing this and that but not surrendering, is not to read it at all, but to compete with it. The loss, in that case, is the reader's because in parts of *Kora* Williams has captured the form of the dreaming mind's motion on the verge of awakening. *Kora in Hell,* which became a source book for his own later writing, and to which he returned frequently for revelations about himself, could become a source book for others as well, a source of energy for poets, a source of misleading information for psychologists, and a source of delight for anyone capable of responding to language in "a state of emergence," where reader and author stand together without preconceptions in a place of pure beginning.

CHAPTER FOUR

Sour Grapes

On February 28, 1921, Edmund Brown of the Four Seas Publishing Company wrote to Williams: "I received the manuscript, 'Picture Poems,' safely. I have not had time to read it entire but there is some great stuff in it" (YALC). Although the book was published as *Sour Grapes*, the working title is indicative of Williams' continuing imagist orientation, long after the movement had waned in Europe. He admits as much: "To me, at that time, a poem was an image, the picture was the important thing. As far as I could, with the material I had, I was lyrical, but I was determined to use the material I knew and much of it did not lend itself to lyricism" (*IWWP*, 35). For Williams, imagism was not a passing fashion but the first instinct of his extraordinarily visual imagination. The first poem he wrote ("a black, black cloud") bears the stamp of it, and even the secondhand writing in his first book suggests a regret that the poet is temporarily "blind to a patent wide reality." Unlike any of the earlier books (even the largely imagistic *Al Que Quiere!*), *Sour Grapes* makes no apology for the exercise of eyesight. Here is the whole poem called "Lines":

> Leaves are grey green,
> the glass broken, bright green.   [*CEP*, 206]

The principles of selection differ from poem to poem. Compare this poem with a strikingly similar one, "Between Walls" (not published until 1938, but possibly written earlier):

        the back wings
        of the

        hospital where
        nothing

        will grow lie
        cinders

        in which shine
        the broken

        pieces of a green
        bottle   [*CEP*, 343]

In both poems the actuality of the green glass is unquestionable; it shines up at you from the page. But although the tone of both descriptions is rigidly impersonal, the poems are far from interchangeable. The presence of leaves in the first poem invites the reader to contrast not just shapes, textures, and color values but two sorts of existence as well, the natural and the artificial, the living and the manufactured, and (by extension) the rural and the urban.[1] The contrast is also implicit in "Between Walls," but because there is no living thing in the poem—just a mockery of the color of growing plants—the feeling of the poem is considerably more sterile and airless. One must not forget, either, that in both poems similarities as well as differences are delicately being posited; the glass is part of a composition, and its color relates to, and also rebounds from, the colors of the leaves or cinders surrounding it. In both poems, the selection and arrangement of the details control the reader's reactions, without any need for comment by the author. In a 1950 notebook, Williams writes:

Always, in a work of art, leave a large part to the imagination of the spectator, thus to arouse his imagination also (never block it) & give him work to do. For that is the prime destination of the thing produced, the created object, the new born infant, to have the beholder through his imagination *take part* in it, thus & only thus to complete it.[2] [YALC]

This statement suggests one of the deeper justifications for Pound's advice never to explain anything, and one that, in *Sour Grapes*, Williams is just beginning to trust.

Perhaps the most important differences between the two poems are structural. In the first, two lines are laid side by side, parallel and equal, like two greens on a canvas. And essentially that is all. The reader will no doubt recall Stevens' "Anecdote of the Jar" or "The Indigo Glass in the Grass," and raise for himself the questions about an artist's arrangements of reality, but he will be doing so on his own. Williams' poem offers no encouragement, it merely presents. In this respect, it is even simpler than this quite similar lyric written at about the same time:

> My luv
> is like
> a
> greenglass
> insulator
> on
> a blue sky

which, after all, contains literary allusion (to Robert Burns) and implicit social comment.[3] The existence of several lyrics about green glass may be significant. One is reminded of the melting bottle in *Paterson*, by which Williams symbolizes among other things the melting of the mind's rigidities during the poetic act. Williams gave the collective title, "Broken

Windows," to eighteen poems that appeared in *Poetry* in 1919 (XIII, 6). And in the Prologue to *Kora in Hell* he wrote: "By the brokenness of his composition the poet makes himself master of a certain weapon which he could possess himself of in no other way" (*Imag.*, 16). At times Williams seems most impressed by the transparency of glass, at times by the invisible barrier it can become between oneself and the world (for instance, the windshield in "Romance Moderne," *CEP*, 181), at times by the way it colors reality, at times by its malleability under heat (metals interest him in this connection, too), or by its jaggedness and jewellike brilliance when broken. At times, it *is* reality for Williams, the hard, glittering imperviousness of a world that poetry can never digest, or leave alone.

Both of these little poems, "My luv" and "Lines," are essentially structureless. To move from them to a poem like "Between Walls" is to move from "Imagism" to "Objectivism," from notations transcribed direct from the mind's retina to a set of built structures (the poem as purring machine, the poem as "object"), which capture whole the imaginative qualities of the objects they describe. "Between Walls" works like the zoom lense of a camera—moving in from the hospital wings to the cinders and finally to the shining edges of glass. The poem's shape contributes to its efficacy, by constantly surprising one's expectations, while at the same time providing a symmetry that will please by retrospect. The word "lie," the primary verb in the poem, serves as the main fulcrum of surprise; its grammatical position makes the reader suddenly wonder if the title should not be read as the first line. Although the poem as a whole moves (that is, zooms in), this verb does not; it is the intransitive conveyor of the subject,

which is itself motionless. The moving focus, the enjambments, the small grammatical surprises excite one's interest
without disturbing the intense quiet; the poem is a motion
picture of a still life.

Hardly any of the poems in *Sour Grapes* make a real attempt at this sort of structural subtlety. In *I Wanted to Write
a Poem*, Williams calls the work "a mood book, all of it impromptu" (34). Although this statement is not strictly true—
in the preceding paragraph, Williams had described two of
the book's "studied" poems—it fairly indicates the work's bias
toward spontaneity of expression as a means of capturing the
immediacy of experience. It is an arguable concept of aesthetics, to be sure, and many artists have achieved the effects
of spontaneity and immediacy only after laborious revisions,
of which the reader is unaware.

In a sense, although Williams showed no great interest in
Eastern mysticism, the differences between the "impromptu"
and the "studied" poems in *Sour Grapes* suggest the differences between Eastern and Western approaches to art. I am
thinking particularly of the Zen art of ink drawing on rice
paper. No erasure is possible, and any hesitation will cause
the brush to go through the paper, destroying the picture. To
learn this art is to learn that improvisation means concentra-
tion-in-motion, one-pointedness moving infallibly and swiftly
across a page, turning into lines that reveal the inner qualities
of the flower, bird, or other object that the artist has chosen.
"*The wish would be to see . . . the imaginative qualities of
the actual things being perceived*," as Williams says of the
improvisations in *Kora in Hell* (*Imag.*, 67). A poem, "imagistic" as it may be, need not attempt to "copy" nature in the
Wyeth manner, but it should "imitate" nature, "imitate what

nature does, for that liberates us by returning us to the imagination."[4]

This remark (made in 1950) about nature is reminiscent of a statement Williams made about Whitman in his first published essay, in 1917: "The only way to be like Whitman is to write *unlike* Whitman."[5] That is, don't mimic his manner, but imitate his poetic action. Breslin puts the matter very well: "Pound, conceding in his famous 'Pact' that Whitman had broken new wood, believed that the modern task was to carve and polish; Williams wanted to re-enact fully the process of release and re-formation that Whitman had started."[6] Whitman was nature for Williams in much the same way that Homer was nature for the poets of the Renaissance; to imitate Homer or Theocritus was merely to follow the laws of nature. But nature has its ups and downs, its seasons, and the mind its moods, and a book of poetry that stays as closely in contact with nature as *Sour Grapes* does will be "definitely a mood book" (*IWWP*, 34). Thus, in that first essay by Williams: "Whitman aside from being the foremost analyst was above all a colorist—a mood man."[7] Tracing accurately the contours of one's moods, then, represents a part of the answer to the implied question: *how* does one follow the "laws of nature" in writing? Another part of the answer is suggested by Thomas R. Whitaker's statement about the "process of thinking *with* things, rather than of them to illustrate thought."[8] To accomplish this feat, one must keep in intimate contact with things, mulling and meditating them till at last one is admitted into their world. If all goes well, the poetry that results will be at once simple and inexplicable; it will convey to the reader "the frightening joy of hearing the world talk to itself."[9]

In December 1920, while Williams was still corresponding

with Edmund Brown about the publication of *Sour Grapes*, the first issue of the magazine *Contact* appeared, edited by Williams and Robert McAlmon. The title pages of the first two issues are laid out in almost exactly the same way as *Others* had arranged its title pages—partly as an acknowledgment of an artistic debt and partly, perhaps, as an indication that the editorial policies of the new magazine would be as open-minded as those of its predecessor. But the differences between the magazines are evident immediately. *Others* was so open-minded that it seemed at times to lack any point of view at all: it merely presented "a blank page to Tom, Dick and Harry with the invitation to write a masterpiece upon it."[10] *Contact*, on the other hand, was cluttered with manifestoes, many of them verbose and filled with jargon, but all of them insisting on the importance to the artist of contact with the local conditions and raw experiences of life.

The first issue concludes with this sentence: "We believe that in the perfection of that contact is the beginning not only of the concept of art among us but the key to the technique also." If the reader gives in to the temptation to dismiss this statement as meaningless, he may be haunted later by the suspicion that he has ignored a profound and germinal clue to a new poetry. Finally, the only way to deal with such advice is to follow it, to see whether the mind's direct contacts with winds and growing trees really do suggest a way for poems to move and grow; to see, also, whether listening to mothers scolding their children or whores cajoling their "Johns" provides any hints about poetic diction and rhetorical movement. A remarkable passage toward the end of the *Autobiography* elaborates this idea almost into mysticism:

The girl who comes to me breathless, staggering into my office, in her underwear a still breathing infant, asking me to lock her

mother out of the room; the man whose mind is gone—all of them
finally say the same thing. And then a new meaning begins to
intervene. For under that language to which we have been listening all our lives a new, a more profound language, underlying
all the dialectics offers itself. It is what they call poetry. That is
the final phase. . . . We begin to see that the underlying meaning of all they want to tell us and have always failed to communicate is the poem, the poem which their lives are being lived
to realize. No one will believe it. And it is the actual words, as
we hear them spoken under all circumstances, which contain it.
[361–362]

This passage and Williams' early editorials are essential to
an understanding of Williams' theory of "contact." From the
first, the ideas of contact and improvisation are closely connected, although their relationship shifts continually. At first,
improvising meant to Williams writing spontaneously, without forethought, as a way of releasing subconscious materials.
In *Sour Grapes* that definition still applies, but the conscious
effort to externalize the viewpoint and to ground it in the
particulars of growing things gives a new quality to the "impromptu" or "improvised" poems in the book. *Kora* alter-
nates the voices of a formal narrator and a disturbed dreamer.
Sour Grapes finds a way outside these mental worlds into the
"real" world. Although in the contrast between the "studied"
and the "impromptu" poems one hears a continuing echo of
the two voices of the earlier book, the reader is in the main
relieved to discover that Williams is no longer self-consciously
mucking about in his own head.

Certainly, the book is not without its share of confusions.
Williams may have suspected that in "contact" lay the key to
technique, but he had not found the most effective ways to
use that key. In any case, the real importance of the book to
Williams' development lies not in structural or prosodic dis-

coveries but in the continuation of the process of inner loosening begun in *The Tempers* and *Al Que Quiere!*, and advanced so dramatically in *Kora in Hell: Improvisations*.

In places there is perhaps too much looseness, too little concentration. In other places, the book shows an opposite tendency. The poem "Overture to a Dance of Locomotives" is overstudied and obscure in ways that require mere figuring out ("dingy cylinders," for instance, stands for railroad cars).[11] Some of the other poems are brilliant in parts and undistinguished in their totalities. "Arrival" starts off with four near-perfect lines:

> And yet one arrives somehow,
> finds himself loosening the hooks of
> her dress
> in a strange bedroom—

The picture of a mind suddenly waking from its automatisms to find itself in a here and now has seldom been more unforgettably drawn. The next three lines, lapsing into easy metaphor, are a letdown:

> feels the autumn
> dropping its silk and linen leaves
> about her ankles.

Williams seems determined to finish this poem somehow. The last lines are a good try:

> The tawdry veined body emerges
> twisted upon itself
> like a winter wind . . . !   [*CEP*, 215]

The eccentric punctuation at the end suggests an embarrassed attempt to hide the poem's inadequacies under the mask of "Spanish" spontaneity (read a silent *Oya!* or *Cesa!* where the three dots stand). Apparently, we learn, the poem's unity is to be achieved by paralleling seasonal change with the woman's disrobing. A clever substitute for a lost inspiration—unworthy of Williams.

Lack of concentration and too much thinking tend to occur within the same poem. The celebrated lyric "The Great Figure" with which Williams concludes *Sour Grapes* is a conveniently short example. Among the correspondence with Edmund Brown there is an early draft of the poem:

> Among the rain
> and lights
> I saw the figure 5
> gold on red
> moving
> to gong clangs
> siren howls
> and wheels rumbling
> tense
> unheeded
> through the dark city[12]   [YALC]

The immediacy of the flashed image seen against a "dark" "rumbling" background is reminiscent of many photographs of Stieglitz's (whom Williams was reportedly on the way to visit when the incident occurred), but the poem itself has no more than a generalized structure. The image convinces, but the choice and order of the words do not. In *Sour Grapes*, there is another version:

> Among the rain
> and lights
> I saw the figure 5
> in gold
> on a red
> firetruck
> moving

```
with weight and urgency
tense
unheeded
to gong clangs
siren howls
and wheels rumbling
through the dark city.
```

This version is better, because "I saw the figure 5 / in gold" is better poetry than "I saw the figure 5/gold on red"; because naming the "firetruck" avoids the aesthetic cuteness of pseudo-impressionism; and because "tense / unheeded" now has a more appropriate noun to modify ("firetruck" instead of "wheels"). The tinkering has resulted in tangible improvements. Still, the poem is structurally a rather loose contraption. Finally, in *The Collected Earlier Poems* (230), there is another version, which deletes the phrase "with weight and urgency." Indeed, its presence in the earlier version had made "tense / unheeded" somewhat redundant. But it is not immediately obvious that, of the two phrases, "tense / unheeded" is the better. In fact, it is weak. "With weight and urgency" functioned in the way the phrase "so much depends" does in "The Red Wheelbarrow," though less subtly—as a humanistic infusion into a realm of impersonal objects. The point is that Williams did not quite "get" the poem in the beginning, and no amount of tinkering could put his vision together again. His brush went through the paper.[13]

Despite structural problems, most of the poems in *Sour Grapes* are successful. The "deft casualness" that Thomas R. Whitaker notices perhaps best characterizes Williams' performance in the collection as a whole and indicates a source of the book's freshness and appeal.[14] The *concerns* of the book might be characterized as those of pastoral poetry. Such an assertion may surprise readers who recall the "fleecy kind" and "finny tribes" of seventeenth- and eighteenth-century pastorals, and for whom the term "pastoral" suggests the word "artificial" rather than the word "natural."[15] But the primary meaning of pastoral, according to Frank Kermode, is "'the antithesis of Art,' the wild or savage as opposed to the cultivated, the material upon which art works. And this opposition is nowhere so evident and acute as in Pastoral, for in this 'kind' the cultivated, in their artificial way, reflect upon and describe, for their own ends, the natural life. . . . Some modern writers use the term 'Pastoral' to describe any work which concerns itself with the contrast between simple and complicated ways of living; its method is to exalt the naturalness and virtue of the simple man at the expense of the complicated one, whether the former be a shepherd, or a child, or a working-man."[16]

By Kermode's definition, the Williams' poem "Lines," which juxtaposes the natural and the artificial, qualifies as a pastoral poem. The term "pastoral" of course must be liberated from the particular conventions that characterized it during Theocritus' or Sidney's time and must be considered instead as a mode of thinking, a generalized set of psychic and literary predilections. A review of Williams' early work reveals a strong pastoral tendency in poems like "First Praise," in *The Tempers,* or in the early "fool's songs," which annoy us today because the peasant narrators are drawn as artificially, if not as skillfully, as the Colin Clouts of traditional pastoral. The same tendency informs a number of poems in *Al Que Quiere!,* most obviously the three which are titled "Pastoral." The simple old man gathering lime, for example, whose bearing is "more majestic than / that of the [citified] Episcopal minister," is Williams' analogue to the shepherd of traditional pastoral poetry.[17] Perhaps the closest literary relation to this poem about the lime gatherer is Wordsworth's poem about a "leech gatherer," an aged mendicant "with many hardships to endure," who yet speaks with a dignity

> . . . above the reach
> Of ordinary men; a stately speech;
> Such as grave Livers do in Scotland use,
> Religious men, who give to God and man their dues.[18]

In his "pastorals," Williams is undoubtedly aware that he is working in a distinguished literary tradition. That fact does not, however, seem to disturb him, perhaps because the tradition happens to correspond to his own modes of thinking and feeling. If pastoral poetry had not existed, Williams would have invented it.

Sour Grapes opens with another implicitly pastoral poem, "The Late Singer," the narrator of which lacks only an oaten flute. Some of the furniture of that poem—the marshes and the sparrows—are not quite "Arcadian" enough for conventional pastoral, and in wicked hands could easily have been turned to clever ironic uses. In fact, pastoral and mock-pastoral, like flattery and satire, are never distant from each other. The idealist is always courting disillusionment; Williams' disillusionment came early, in the experience cryptically allegorized in "The Wanderer." After that he sometimes tried irony, but he was never much good at it. His disillusionment kept healing, and the childlike innocence of sight kept returning. The brown sparrow is no skylark, and the marsh no meadow, but "The Late Singer" is free from any tinge of satire. Having died out of his old ideals of a remote perfection and beauty, Williams discovered that beauty had suddenly become abundantly available to him. It was literally everywhere, even, he would discover, "by the road to the contagious hospital."

The longer "Romance Moderne," toward the beginning of *Sour Grapes*, also expresses pastoral concerns, the nature / civilization dichotomy in particular. The first three stanzas lay out the traditional conflict and the proposed resolution:

Tracks of rain and light linger in
the spongy greens of a nature whose
flickering mountain—bulging nearer,
ebbing back into the sun
hollowing itself away to hold a lake,—
or brown stream rising and falling
at the roadside, turning about,
churning itself white, drawing
green in over it,—plunging glassy funnels
fall—

And—the other world—
the windshield a blunt barrier:
Talk to me. Sh! they would hear us.
—the backs of their heads facing us—
The stream continues its motion of
a hound running over rough ground.

Trees vanish—reappear—vanish:
detached dance of gnomes—as a talk
dodging remarks, glows and fades.
—The unseen power of words—
And now that a few of the moves
are clear the first desire is
to fling oneself out at the side into
the other dance, to other music.   [*CEP*, 181]

Here is a poem which, like the equally long "History," is neither a simple impromptu nor a belabored pastiche. It holds a taut line throughout, balancing perfectly over the two worlds it describes. The concentration of the language results in the same sorts of obscurity that characterize the best parts of *Kora in Hell*—not the obscurity of recondite metaphor (as in "Overture to a Dance of Locomotives"), but the obscurity of subliminal realities seized by "the eye awake!" as he puts it later in the poem. Simple versus sophisticated love, the desire to merge with the world of nature ("to fling oneself out at the side into / the other dance"), the contrast between an animistic nature ("bulging," "hollowing," "churning," "drawing . . . in," "plunging") and the "blunt barrier" behind which civilization hides—these are all the concerns of Williams' brand of neopastoral poetry.

The four long flower poems, "Daisy," "Primrose," "Queen-Ann's-Lace," and "Great Mullen," also have a pastoral flavor. As Kermode explains, "Flowers were valued not only as decorations for the laureate hearse of a dead shepherd-poet, but for their own beauty. Although, in thoughtful mood, the poet might think of Nature as God's Book of the Creatures, the more usual reaction of the Elizabethan poet is one of spontaneous pleasure."[19] The feeling of pleasure is certainly Williams' reaction as well, but the intensity and intimacy of his contact with the flowers he describes carries him beyond the animistic naturalism of his earlier flower poems ("Chickory and Daisies," for instance) into a state of almost hallucinatory identification, in which figures of myth, unnamed, begin to move again. For Williams, flowers have always held deep meanings. In the *Autobiography*, he speaks of his "personal wild world" just over the back fence and of "a half-ashamed pleasure" he felt as a child in playing the naturalist. "My curiosity in these things was unbounded—secret, certainly. There is a long history in each of us that comes as not only a re-awakening but a repossession when confronted by this world.

To look up and see on a tree blooms, yellow and green . . .
was something astonishing to me. . . . I was comforted by
them. . . . just to know the flowers was all I wanted"
(19–20). Later, he speaks of "my particular secret place."
"This is my first memory of the odor of violets" (31). "The
green-flowered asphodel made a tremendous impression on
me. I collected all such flowers . . . and pressed them between the leaves of a copybook" (29). The secrecy of his activities and their apparent sacredness are intriguing. The flowers pressed between the leaves of a copybook when Williams
was twelve and thirteen are psychological homologues to the
Leaves of Grass poems ("my secret life," he calls them) he
wrote into copybooks when he was eighteen and nineteen.
The fact that Whitman himself wrote many poems about
common New England flowers—mullen, for example—may
have supplied a further psychic connection between collect-
ing and writing. Flowers, poems, and women are closely in-
terrelated for Williams. All three represent perfect beauty,
contain secrets and generative mysteries, and combine deli-
cacy with great hardiness and power ("Saxifrage is my flower
that splits / the rocks," *CLP*, 7). "Somehow poetry and the
female sex were allied in my mind," he says of his earliest
work (*IWWP*, 14). "Two women. Three women. / Innumerable women, each like a flower" (*Pat.*, 15). "Are facts not
flowers / and flowers facts / or poems flowers / or all works
of the imagination, / interchangeable?" (*PFB*, 178).[20]
    In the anthology, *Others for 1919*, Williams published
seven flower poems under the title "Flowers of August," including three of the four that later appeared in *Sour Grapes*.
The fourth, "Primrose," did not appear in the anthology, perhaps because the primrose is not a flower of August, or per-

haps because the poem was written after the others. Together, these eight poems constitute a suite of independent but not unrelated improvisations, often as obscure and as expostulatory as those in *Kora*. The difference is that in *Kora* Williams lets one thing lead to another and to another, often without returning to the point of departure, whereas in the group of flower poems there is always the object—a daisy, a thistle, a healall—being held under relentless scrutiny, so that, even though one association leads randomly to the next, collectively the associations circle the object of their concern. The daisy is examined from the front and then from the rear, where "brownedged, / green and pointed scales / armor his yellow." Thus, although half-personified male and female principles roam the poems, the reader never gets really lost. The almost medical thoroughness of the examination and the intensity of the poet's emotion toward the plant he is considering lead at times to an imagined merging of their consciousness. In "Thistle," for example, "Our heads side by side have a purple / flamebed over them. We are one, we love / ourself. The cows do not eat us nor tread / on us."[21]

One's feelings about these poems tend to be mixed. "Great Mullen," for instance, starts beautifully:

> One leaves his leaves at home
> being a mullen and sends up a lighthouse
> to peer from: I will have my way,
> yellow—

But later it becomes so querulously obscure that the reader feels quite left out:

> She has had her
> hand on you!—well?—She has defiled
> ME.—Your leaves are dull, thick

and hairy.—Every hair on my body will
hold you off from me. You are a
dungcake, birdlime on a fencerail.—[*CEP*, 211]

Who is this "she" that keeps appearing in these poems? The
sun perhaps, or Kora, the female fertility principle. But although "she" had a very real meaning for Williams and indi-
cated her presence through every woman whom he helped
through labor pains, she is most efficacious as a Muse when
she stays in the background of his poetry. Perhaps the most
successful of the flower poems is "Primrose," in which no
uses of "she," "he," or even "we" are to be found at all:

Yellow, yellow, yellow, yellow!
It is not a color.
It is summer!
It is the wind on a willow,
the lap of waves, the shadow
under a bush, a bird, a bluebird,
three herons, a dead hawk
rotting on a pole—
Clear yellow!
It is a piece of blue paper
in the grass or a threecluster of
green walnuts swaying, children
playing croquet or one boy
fishing, a man
swinging his pink fists
as he walks—
It is ladysthumb, forget-me-nots
in the ditch, moss under
the flange of the carrail, the
wavy lines in split rock, a
great oaktree—
It is a disinclination to be
five red petals or a rose, it is
a cluster of birdsbreast flowers

on a red stem six feet high,
four open yellow petals
above sepals curled
backward into reverse spikes—
Tufts of purple grass spot the
green meadow and clouds the sky.   [*CEP*, 209]

The first thing that strikes one is the excited repetition of the
color-word, "yellow!" The second is the immediate contra-
diction, "It is not a color." Williams uses verbal doubling back
to sensational effect throughout the poem and in fact throughout the collection. His earlier repudiation of the artificial de-
vices used in *Poems* (1909) had led him to a diction that was
often prosy and flat, and whose lack of pressure no amount of
exclamation could disguise. The use of verbal repetition for
rhythmical effects in *Sour Grapes* is a sign of Williams' readiness to reintroduce, in fact reinvent, lyricism in his lines. The
repetition of particular words and syntactic forms, joined with
the repetition of key sounds, produces in the reader the illu-
sion of a physical sensation, such as one may experience while
watching a dancer and empathizing with his or her movements. One has the same sensation reading the last few lines
of "The Cold Night":

In April . . .
In April I shall see again—In April!
the round and perfect thighs
of the Police Sergeant's wife
perfect still after many babies.
Oya!   [*CEP*, 203]

As always when he is at his best, Williams manages to steer
the poem away from mere flatness on the one hand, and stilted
diction on the other. In "Primrose," what could have been
merely a list becomes in his hands an incantation, all of it kept

fresh and a bit mysterious by the apparent contradictions: "Clear yellow! / It is a piece of blue paper."

The poem invites one to contemplate the spectacle of a lexicographer gone mad, for it plays with the idea of establishing adequate definitions for words—here, the entry is "primrose"—and concludes, after considering some twenty-two synonyms, that the task is endless, perhaps absurd. As in the book as a whole, there is implicit comedy beneath the genuine excitement of this poem, comedy which is easier to experience than to explain, as one discovers when one tries to analyze the perfection of Williams' choice of the placid Latinism in the lines, "It is a disinclination to be / five red petals or a rose." The poem has a great deal in common with the more overtly comic "Portrait of a Lady" (published in 1920, but not in *Sour Grapes*), which also investigates the plight of words in collision with actuality. And again Williams' autobiographical statements are misleading. In *I Wanted to Write a Poem*, he says of his work at this time, "All the poems are poems of disappointment, sorrow. I felt rejected by the world" (33). His writing had not met with any commercial success, but the poems in *Sour Grapes* are not sorrowful—regardless of their subject matter. They are subversive and confident and totally lacking in illusions. The mood they reflect is not a bad one for an artist. The restlessness of feeling oneself on the brink of something new causes some artists to push through to their finest achievements.

CHAPTER FIVE

Spring and All

Williams' obsessive discussion in *Spring and All* (1923) of the different functions and qualities of prose and poetry brings new clarity to the processes of the five books that precede it. Ruling out the usual schoolroom distinctions between prose and poetry, Williams concludes that the real difference lies in the fact that prose and poetry have different psychic origins, "each using similar modes for dis-similar purposes; verse falling most commonly into meter but not always, and prose going forward most often without meter but not always" (*Imag.*, 144). "Prose, relieved of extraneous, unrelated values must return to its only purpose[:] to clari[f]y[,] to enlighten the understanding. There is no form to prose but that which depends on clarity. If prose is not accurately adjusted to the exposition of facts it does not exist—Its form is that alone. . . . Poetry is something quite different. Poetry has to do with the crystallization of the imagination—the perfection of new forms as additions to nature" (*Imag.*, 140). Prose, then, is to poetry as fact is to "imaginative reality" (*Imag.*, 135). This latter term is not easy to define, and Williams does not succeed in defining it, though he makes valiant attempts. To see something of what he means, though, one might turn back to *Kora in Hell* and note the real differences, in purpose as well as method, between the italicized and non-italicized paragraphs. The distinction can be seen less subtly in *Spring and All*, in which an obviously discursive prose is placed against a conventionally notated poetry. Not that the poetry itself is "conventional"; in fact, reading it forces one again to question the prose/poetry distinction, and to ask how "prosy" a poem can be and still be poetry. Williams claims that his own ear has by this time become so finely tuned that he can read Whitman and tell what lines are poetry, what lines bad poetry, and what lines prose. Unfortunately, he does not give examples.

Anyone who seriously writes poetry and some who read it have sensed that moment when words, which were just words, begin to acquire a sheen or patina, an electricity; Williams refers to it often in *Kora* as the dance of the imagination over the page. Pursuing the matter in *Spring and All*, Williams offers a sentence for discussion: "Tomorrow will be the first of April." He comments:

> Certainly there is an emotional content in this for anyone living in the northern temperate zone, but whether it is prose or poetry—taken by itself—who is going to say unless some mark is put on it by the intent conveyed by the words which surround it—
> Either to write or to comprehend poetry the words must be recognized to be moving in a direction separate from the jostling or lack of it which occurs within the piece. [*Imag.*, 146]

What that "mark" is, and where that separate direction leads, are mysteries that do not yield to critical formulations, not even Williams'. Significantly, this prose section is followed immediately by the most deliberate challenge so far in the book to the reader's ability to discern the "mark" of poetry on the words: a poem composed entirely of clichés, traffic signs, bits of conversation, and advertisements. It begins, "Somebody dies every four minutes / in New York State—." Among the inhospitable lines that glare up defiantly at the reader are the following:

> Careful Crossing Campaign
> Cross Crossings Cautiously.   [*Imag.*, 146]

If you can't see the mark here, Williams seems to be saying, you won't see it in Shakespeare, though you'll think you do. As Pound once said, "One wonders what the devil anyone will make of this sort of thing who has not in his wit all the clues."[1] *Spring and All* posits a Whitmanlike inclusiveness ("We are one. Whenever I say, 'I' I mean also, 'you.' " *Imag.*, 89). But the book is essentially for other writers, for those who already have the clues.

Even for poets, coming at Williams' meaning is a process more often of pursuing inferences than of ingesting immediately usable information. Unable to speak of the imagination in the definitive language of science, Williams is forced (like everyone else) to employ figurative language, which, by the time of *Spring and All*, he has taught his readers to distrust as "an easy lateral sliding" (*Imag.*, 14). Williams avoids some of the dangers of metaphorical definition by using a number of metaphors, each of which partially cancels out the others, leaving one simply with a lively sense of what he is "getting at."

Once decoded, his description of the imagination and of the ways that poets can avail themselves of it in their writing may be seen in its full importance. Central to his thinking about poetry is the idea of freedom. Words are either free or they are bound, either clean or smeared (with historical overtones, symbolic implications, metaphorical associations). Yet "contact" is also important; a word cannot be "freed" from its obligations to the object it depicts. In fact, a word gains its freedom *through* the object which gives it reality. (For some ramifications of this statement, see *Imag.*, 150.)

In some places he describes the imagination as a force, in others as a place. Often he sees it as an active transforming agent, dynamizing facts into realities; sometimes he sees it as an immobile element in a shifting world: it "stands still . . . and forces change about itself—sifting the world for permanence, in the drift of nonentity" (*Imag.*, 134). What principle of selection does this straining process involve? Why should one fact contain more potential for permanence than another? An answer is to be found in another of Williams' images, that of a stone being hurled through a beautiful rose window, and fragments of colored glass following the stone in a stream (as a slow-motion camera will reveal that they do). The principle of selection is not worth pondering because the process is automatic: those facts, images, and sentence fragments that are most directly affected by the impact of the imagination upon reality will follow the poem's trajectory, forming a perfect hieroglyph of escape:

> Clean is he alone
> after whom stream
> the broken pieces of the city—   [*Imag.*, 115]

But for the imagination to act instantly, as it must, it has to be roused and kept in a state of readiness. At one point in *The Great American Novel*, a work of experimental prose published the same year as *Spring and All*, Williams says, "It fell by chance on his ear but he was ready, he was alert" (*Imag.*, 171). If the imagination is in the attic and the body is in the cellar, a man cannot act with the instinctive speed

which is as necessary to Williams' new-found objectivism as
it is to the Zen master's drawing on rice paper, or to the action painting of Jackson Pollock, of which Williams may be
considered a spiritual forerunner. "It is necessary to dwell in
the imagination if the truth is to be numbered. It is necessary
to speak from the imagination" (*Imag.*, 112). The imagination must therefore be centered in the body, and the body
itself be roused, susceptible to outside influence.[2] The poem
will then explode into existence the moment its occasion arises.

Williams did not arrive at this "somatic" view of the poem
through any linear theoretical process; the seed was in him
from the beginning, as early as his first subversive fascination
with Whitman. The first poem he wrote "was born like a
bolt out of the blue. It came unsolicited" (*Auto.*, 47). "At
once, at the same instant, I said to myself, 'Ridiculous, the rain
can't drive the clouds.' So the critical thing was being born
at the same time" (*IWWP*, 4). Apollo and Dionysus both
spoke to him at once, and the two voices have echoed through
his writing ever since, conflicting vectors whose resultant has
frequently been astonishing poetry. The sense of duality is
behind almost all his statements about poetry and the imagination. Poe, for instance, "could not have written a word without the violence of expulsive emotion combined with the in-
driving force of a crudely repressive environment. Between
the two his imagination was forced into being" (*Imag.*, 111).
In a sense, Williams' decision to juxtapose *himself* to an
uncongenial environment all his life, instead of fleeing like
James, Eliot, Pound, and others, is evidence of his recognition
of the creative force that can be generated by the collision
of antagonistic elements. The decision to stay in Rutherford,
New Jersey, was no doubt a difficult one. In *Poems*, the repressive literary environment won a total, if temporary, vic-

tory over him; but in Williams' later work, propriety and spontaneity, "Keats" and "Whitman," lost some of their qualities as moral opposites and began interacting in ways that Williams found aesthetically fruitful, if one may judge by his fondness for juxtaposing them.

A major difference between the poems in *Spring and All* and those in *Sour Grapes* is that in the earlier book formal considerations and spontaneity tend to be segregated—there are "studied" poems and "impromptu" poems—whereas in *Spring and All* the attempt is to fuse the two and to make form instinctive. In this task readiness is all, and the poet must be constantly in training, like an athlete. "I do not smoke since it drugs the intelligence," he wrote early in 1919; "I want all my reactions. I do not drink except for the taste; I despise the lurid vapors of alcohol."[3] The only unit of poetic time is the moment, and one must avoid everything that "distracts the attention from its agonized approaches to the moment" (*Imag.*, 89). Whitaker cites a manuscript in which Williams claims to have written "The Red Wheelbarrow" in two minutes' time. What is surprising is that it took as *long* as that. Yet Whitaker feels he must defend Williams, saying that this fact "does not diminish [the poem's] importance. It testifies to the ability to record at the moment of enlarged and focused consciousness. Writing as revelation, Williams later said, consists of 'the most complicated formulas worked out . . . in a few seconds and set down' (*SE*, 268f)."[4] By the time of *Spring and All*, perfection of form and speed of composition may almost be considered functions of each other. If Williams had tinkered with "The Red Wheelbarrow," he would have botched it, as he did "The Great Figure" in *Sour Grapes*. "Here's a man wants me to revise . . . ," he writes in *The Great American Novel*. "My

God what I am doing means just the opposite from that. There is no revision, there can be no revision—" (*Imag.*, 176). The aim of this approach to composition is to produce "new forms as additions to nature" (*Imag.*, 140). The pretentiousness of this announced aim is tempered by the reality of the psychological need which underlies it. One cannot dispute Williams' contention that "life becomes actual only when it is identified with ourselves" (*Imag.*, 115). The strongly inhibited childhood and adolescence (lasting well into his twenties) that Williams underwent no doubt greatly increased the need to make his life "actual" to himself. To accomplish this he tried to uncover his cultural origins, to explore genealogical leads, and to identify as closely as he could with the locality in which he found himself. In his poetry, he tried to "become" the objects he describes. His intent was not to "describe" at all, but to fuse the imagination with the things he was contemplating so that his words would "express" those objects, almost speak for them. He seems actually to have believed that, when successful (that is, when dynamized by the imagination), the poem will behave in accordance with natural law and so will become an "addition to nature," another object under the sun.

Paradoxically, in becoming a natural object the poem becomes separate from nature. A poem about a certain Rutherford sycamore, for instance, may take on all the reality of a thing among things, but it will not *be* the sycamore tree. Least of all will it be a "description" of the sycamore tree. "Not 'realism' but reality itself" (*Imag.*, 117). A separate reality.

Williams was not the only one to think of art in these terms, nor was he the first, as his frequent references to the writings of Marsden Hartley and Juan Gris suggest. The advent of Cubism signaled a great liberation, not just for painters, but equally for writers and even for musicians. In 1925, Gris wrote: "Cubism is not a manner but an aesthetic; and even a state of mind; it is therefore inevitably connected with every manifestation of contemporary thought."[5]

One of the poems in *Spring and All*, beginning "The rose is obsolete," is apparently a verbal transcription of a 1914 Gris collage, "Roses." Bram Dijkstra's discussion of the poem and the painting (*Hieroglyphics*, 173–176) accurately notes the qualities of hardness and precision in both works, and the absence of any symbolic overlay. Each petal in both the painting and the poem is discrete, almost metallically so:

> Somewhere the sense
> makes copper roses
> steel roses—   [*Imag.*, 108]

In *Sour Grapes*, Williams had already attained a measure of detached precision, particularly in the poem "Daisy":

> the crisp petals remain
> brief, translucent, greenfastened,
> barely touching at the edges:
> blades of limpid seashell.   [*CEP*, 208]

But there was still the faint overlay of allegory, a "he" and a "she," and even a loud "ha!" from Williams' gypsy alter ego. A measure of the change that had taken place is the fact that in *Sour Grapes* the most common mark of punctuation is the exclamation point, whereas in *Spring and All* it is the dash. In the poems in the latter book there are only three exclamation points.

The prose in *Spring and All* is frequently emphatic, even aphoristic, but the poems, grammatically at least, avoid conclusions. Like his uncle, Carlos Hoheb, who combined the "opposites" of Spaniard and scientist, Williams in this book maintains a strict balance. He is consciously the scientist of words, laying them together with great care in order to point up both the autonomy of each image and the sensuous, "painterly" geometry of the relationships between the images.

In an essay on Marianne Moore written not long after *Spring and All*, Williams isolates two essential elements, "the hard and unaffected concept of the apple itself as an idea, then its edge-to-edge contact with the things which surround it . . . and without connectives" (*Imag.*, 315). The sharp edges of Williams' rose petals are in direct contact with nothing but the air. But the air, for anyone infected with Cubism, is far from nothing: each petal *cements* "the grooved columns of air" and starts a line which, "infinitely fine, infinitely / rigid penetrates / the Milky Way" (*Imag.*, 108). Robert Burns' red red rose is obsolete, but the rose itself and the painting and the poem are each autonomous and eternal, separate and equal.

This separateness is balanced by the necessary second element, contact. Even if the contact is only with air, a relationship is set up. Almost always, though, there are other objects within the vicinity created by the painter's or poet's frame. In Gris' collage there is a newspaper, a vase, dishes, the silhouette of a pipe. Each object has been fragmented, but there is a visual relationship uniting them all; the fragment is part of a visual flow. Since this duality exactly corresponds to the paradox inherent in Williams' own life, it is easy to see why Cubism, particularly in its "synthetic" stage, held a strong attraction for him. His rose petal, like Gris', "meets— nothing—renews / itself in metal or porcelain—":

> whither? It ends—
>
> But if it ends
> the start is begun

> so that to engage roses
> becomes a geometry—
>
> Sharper, neater, more cutting
> figured in majolica—
> the broken plate
> glazed with a rose   [*Imag.*, 107–108]

This is careful writing, each line a broken fragment marked with its own distinctive insignia, with which Williams weaves his poem. He is not above a good pun ("whither? It ends—"), or a seeming tautology ("the start is begun"), so long as each line seems new-minted, with its own "patina" or "glaze." This last word, of course, shines with particular significance from its place of incandescence in the famous wheelbarrow poem. Its function there as well as in the rose poem suggests a mind more likely to be startled by Cubistic particulars than to be wooed by impressionistic blurs, even blurs of genius.

When Williams said the crossroads was his home, he was accepting, among other bisections, the one spoken of by Gris in his talk "On the Possibilities of Painting":

> Painting for me is like a fabric, all of a piece and uniform, with one set of threads as the representational, aesthetic element, and the crossthreads as the technical, architectural, or abstract element. . . .
> The role of aesthetic analysis is to break down the material world, in order to select from it elements of the same category.
> Technique should serve to elaborate all these formal elements into a coherent unity. Its role is synthetic.[6]

The vertical and the horizontal, the male and the female, the breaking and the mending, the aesthetic (a strict selectivity) and the technique (the weaving of the selected elements into a unified poem or painting), these are all parallel if somewhat mythological terms, with correlatives on every level of the psyche. There are limitations, of course, to meta-phorical comparisons. Some artists, perhaps Williams among them, might prefer to put technique on the "vertical" or "male" side of the scale and aesthetic on the "horizontal," "female" side. It hardly matters, not at least in works like *Spring and All,* in which aesthetic and technique approach each other's domain so closely that they seem to exchange properties.

The aesthetic concepts held by Gris and Williams are so similar that it is sometimes revealing to examine a Williams proclamation (for example, the imagination "sift[s] the world for permanence") in the light of a statement by Gris (for example, "Aesthetic analysis . . . select[s] from [the world] elements of the same category"). Comparisons with state-ments by other artists of the period elucidate the theory even further. Pierre Reverdy, a French "Cubist" poet and a friend of Gris, wrote, "The characteristic of the strong image is that it results from the spontaneous bringing together of two very remote realities whose connection has been grasped *by the spirit alone.*"[7] Assuming an approximate identity in these three statements of the terms "imagination," "aesthetic analy-sis," and "spirit," it is possible to construct a fairly coherent aesthetic argument—perhaps even to resolve the apparent con-tradictions in Williams' statements about art.

In *Spring and All,* speaking of the improvisations in *Kora,* Williams confesses that "their fault is their dislocation of sense, often complete" (*Imag.,* 117). In a later work, called *Novelette* (and in a chapter titled "Juan Gris"), he speaks of the improvisations again, declaring that "their excellence is, in major part, the shifting of category. It is the disjointing process" (*Imag.,* 285). Unless there is some hidden distinction between dislocating and disjointing which makes one a fault and the other a virtue, one must look to Reverdy and Gris for a key that turns. In some of the improvisations, apparently, the juxtaposed realities were too remote to be bridged even by the "spirit." In others that bridging was possible—that is, the remote realities contained "elements of the same category," albeit a nonlogical category—and the disjointing process became a distinct virtue. Shifting categories, sliding the context out from under the feet of common realities, was a method by which Williams and the painters he admired attempted to "make it new." Take the context of romantic love away from the rose and you have freed the rose to be what it is, as Stein perceived so aphoristically. Supply the rose with a new context and you have freed it even from the necessity by which nature plagiarizes itself. As Reverdy writes: "It is only in that moment when words are freed from their literal meaning that they take on in the mind a poetic value. It is at that moment that they can be freely placed in the poetic reality."[8] The words might as easily have been written by Williams.

It is likely that Williams and Reverdy never heard of each other. Yet from different sides of the hemisphere both shared in the remarkable community of ideas that influenced not just painters and writers but also architects such as Le Corbusier and composers such as Stravinsky.[9] The artists working their revolutions in the early decades of the century tended to view themselves as craftsmen, as daring artisans, rather than as painters and composers in the old "grand" sense. They were scientists of technique, who, freeing themselves from epic intentions, began to analyze the structures of actuality, the nature of their materials, and the contents of their private emotions. The work of art was something to set going, to get off

the ground, like a Wright brothers' plane. Experimentation
with structure, selection of "elements of the same category,"
regardless of the relative "nobility" of the category, replaced
the quest for beauty for its own sake.

The removal of mental build-up from the surfaces of reality revealed a new and unexpected beauty beneath. Artists
examined the mechanics of nature and learned the nature of
mechanics. One should not be misled then, reading in Williams' introduction to *The Wedge* (1944) that "a poem is a
small (or large) machine made of words" (*SE, 256*). His intention is not to deny the relation of the poem to the shapes
and processes of nature but to stress the poem's power, self-
sufficiency, and economy. In fact, he speaks of nature itself
in the same "mechanical" terms:

Oh damn loveliness. Poets have written of the big leaves and the
little leaves, leaves that are red, green, yellow and the one thing
they have never seen about a leaf is that it is a little engine. It is
one of the things that make a plant GO.[10]

With some exceptions, the poems in *Spring and All* "go"
in ways that his earlier poems could not, because of an incompleteness in their structure. Take, for instance, poem XI,
later titled "The Right of Way":

brief images one
might see while
driving

> In passing with my mind
> on nothing in the world
>
> but the right of way
> I enjoy on the road by
>
> virtue of the law   —
> I saw
>
> an elderly man who
> smiled and looked away

emptly
daydream
Freeze Frame

Taking Notice of little things in life
(inconsequential
Mundane

to the north past a house—
a woman in blue

who was laughing and
leaning forward to look up

into the man's half
averted face

and a boy of eight who was
looking at the middle of

the man's belly
at a watchchain—

The supreme importance
of this nameless spectacle

sped me by them
without a word—

Why bother where I went?
for I went spinning on the

four wheels of my car
along the wet road until

I saw a girl with one leg
over the rail of a balcony   [*Imag.*, 119–120]

If there is a flaw in the structure of this poem, it may be found in the lines, "The supreme importance / of this nameless spectacle," which are not nearly so concise as the famous opening, "so much depends / upon," and which remind one of certain mildly uncomfortable tag lines from earlier poems.

The way to avoid having to justify the importance of an image would be to find a significant image to begin with. As Williams himself perceives, "The insignificant 'image' may be 'evoked' never so ably and still mean nothing" (*Imag.*, 101).

[handwritten margin notes: "Events in Life"; "Jolt that everyone has troubles in life"]

The problem is that one man's insignificance may be another's portent. Richard Brautigan has a fine little takeoff on Imagism, Eastern style, called "Haiku Ambulance":[11]

> A piece of green pepper
> fell
> off the wooden salad bowl:
> so what?

Green peppers are not, of course, inherently comic or aesthetically undesirable. One thinks of that famous and extremely sensuous photograph of peppers by Edward Weston. The point is that, if Brautigan had chosen to see his subject not as trivial but as extremely beautiful and important, he too might have been forced to assert its importance in some way: "so much depends / upon / a green pepper." One's only hope is to be subtle and to apply only so much moral pressure on the image as is needed and no more.

In many of the earlier poems, the importance of an image is asserted primarily to justify having used the image; the assertion has no structural function in itself. But in the poem "The Right of Way," the justifying phrase serves as a pivot on which to swing the attention from that static, twelve-line "photograph" (lines seven through eighteen) forward to the resumed action ("sped me by them").

Although it seems unfortunate that Williams had to assert the *supreme* importance of his brief experience, some compensation may be found in his allowing the experience to remain nameless. One is reminded of that crucial letter to Marianne Moore (*SL*, 147): "Things have no names for me. . . . As a reward for this anonymity I feel as much a part of things as trees and stones." Perhaps filmmaker Stan Brakhage had a similar feeling when he remarked, "I am not I when I see."

The thing perceived invades the perceiving consciousness and overmasters it. For the poet it is a temporary death, and eye for an I for which there is no remedy but the speed of time and space. There is no poetic justice but the poem.

Breslin contends that in *Spring and All* "what Williams gives us is a continuous process of surrender and assertion— the way to a renewed individuality."[12] The justness of this remark can be seen not only in the format of the book but equally in the inner processes of some of the poems, including "The Right of Way." The poet who writes in order "to have nothing in my head" (*SE*, 101) begins his poem, "In passing with my mind / on nothing in the world / but the right of way." This state of passive vulnerability, of empty daydream, is the necessary precondition to the profound, if brief, dying into life that is to follow. Already in the midst of the poem, the poet sees his subject and surrenders to it completely for twelve lines of great static tension: three figures looking in three different directions, as if posed by an emblem-maker who wished to capture in one design the whole history of one family's relationships, tragic, tender, hopeful, inarticulate, mutually isolated, mutually dependent. One is reminded of the central scaffold scene in *The Scarlet Letter*, in which Dimmesdale, Hester, and little Pearl stand together in a symbolic configuration as resonantly poignant as it is artificial. So powerfully is the poet affected, that he returns to his own life as if waking from a dream, completely distracted ("Why bother where I went?"), until, marvelously, a minute later he is overpowered by another vision of actuality in transcendence: "I went spinning on the / four wheels of my car / along the wet road until / I saw a girl with one leg / over the rail of a balcony."

The poem helps one to see what Williams means by the imagination's power to sift the "world for permanence, in the drift of nonentity" (*Imag.*, 134). For some reason, the sight of the girl swinging her leg over the rail of a balcony—that detail alone—struck the imagination of the poet with great force. One may speculate about the implicit and perhaps unconscious sensuality of the girl's position, that indolence of incipient womanhood that tantalized Williams as much as it did Yeats (or Humbert Humbert, for that matter); but one cannot finally say why his imagination sifted out just those details, or why a red wheelbarrow "glazed" with rainwater impressed him so deeply. Probably he himself could not satisfactorily explain these matters.

In assessing Williams' great influence on younger poets, most critics focus on the later works, those employing the famous "variable foot." But the earlier poems, particularly those in *Spring and All*, have been equally influential. Compare the poem under discussion with this, by A. R. Ammons:[13]

WCW

I turned in
by the bayshore
and parked,
the crosswind
hitting me hard
side the head,
the bay scrappy
and working:
what a
way to read
Williams! till
a woman came
and turned

            her red dog loose
            to sniff
            (and piss
            on)
            the dead horseshoe
            crabs.

In the sparest of plain language, a first person singular becomes completely absorbed in the scene he is witnessing. Instead of Williams' freeze-frame vision of the man, woman,
and watch-chained boy, one is shown a kinetic, "movie" version of a windy bay. Then the value judgment, the stepping
in: "what a / way to read / Williams!" As in the case of Williams' less subtle intrusion ("The supreme importance / of
this nameless spectacle"), Ammons' explicit emotional valua-
tion serves as a structural pivot, just as waking up from one
trance makes possible entering another: Ammons: "till a
woman came / and turned / her red dog loose." Williams:
"until / I saw a girl with one leg / over the rail of a balcony."
    The implicit advice in these poems is to be one of those on
whom, in James' phrase, "nothing is lost." Williams' work
suggests a variant of the American obsession to possess the
environment, to wrest from it its secrets and powers. There
are two ways to possess America: the way of Cortez, the con-
queror, whose spiritual descendants are now strip-mining in
Kentucky (see "The Destruction of Tenochtitlan," *IAG*,
27–38); and the way of De Soto, who came to conquer but,
in Williams' interpretation, was conquered himself by the
female spirit of the New World ("De Soto and the New
World," *IAG*, 45–58). Possession by surrender, it might be
called. The advice of the poems in *Spring and All* is to open
one's sensibilities to the world, and when the world presents
one (as it will) with some unexpected and unexplainable per-

fection, to record only those details that *most* strike one. By learning this obedience, this self-abnegating submission to the wisdom of astonishment, a poet may write an occasional poem that "knows" and says more than he knows or could say in his own person. One suspects that Williams did not write the wheelbarrow poem so much as he *gave in* to it. No one denies the subtlety of the poem's structure; Eli Siegel and other critics have belabored the artistry of that little poem to the point of apotheosis. But by the time Williams came to write that poem, he was at the point he had boasted (too early) to Viola Baxter about having reached in 1914: "I reduce myself to tinder that when the flash comes I respond totally" (YALC).

This sort of flame is not one that would be expected to burn uninterruptedly through a long poetic work. It is a lyricism that flares and then must be rekindled by some new occasion. Yet Williams was always concerned with the long poem, from his early *Endymion* imitation through the last book of *Paterson*. Ultimately, he found that by constantly juxtaposing his "two selves," his two inner voices, and by adopting a three-step line based on the principle of the "variable foot," he could sustain a poem for a considerable time (though even in these longer works there is a continual "rekindling" from section to section). Much critical effort has been expended in demonstrating the unity of Williams' large poetic structures, but readers without a vested interest in the matter may find that these longer works tend, for the most part, to break apart in their hands, leaving them with a collection of lyrics interspersed with paragraphs of prose.

In places, though, *Spring and All* makes exciting approaches to a structural unity, particularly where the reader is made to feel the ebb and flow of the "continual process of surrender and assertion," as Breslin puts it. He continues: "By a characteristically circular process Williams empties his mind in order to fill it. Importantly, he makes clear here that creative activity, which begins by subverting rational activity, ends by renewing it."[14] This process of alternation is what propels *Kora in Hell*, and it provides much of the combustion for *Spring and All*. A long prose passage of excited exposition will leave the poet at the doorstep of a poem; a poem's imaginative reordering of reality will give rise to a burst of speculation as to what has just occurred and what else is needed. A strange expectancy fills the brief silence between the end of the following prose passage and the beginning of the poem:

> Now at last that process of miraculous verisimilitude, that great copying which evolution has followed, repeating move for move every move that it made in the past—is approaching the end.
> Suddenly it is at an end. THE WORLD IS NEW.

> I
>
> By the road to the contagious hospital
> under the surge of the blue
> mottled clouds driven from the
>
> northeast— [*Imag.*, 95]

No matter how impassioned, lyrical, rhythmical the prose, its voice is different from that of the poetry, and the moment of transition, when the assertive intellect yields to the imagination, is as magical as the analogous moment in a symphony when the tempo suddenly shifts and all the instruments get out of the way before the entrance of an unaccompanied violin. Octavio Paz has called poetry "the other language." In *Spring and All*, the continuous contrasts between the expository and the lyric modes lend an almost incontrovertible authority to this simple definition.

One might argue that *Spring and All* does not fail structurally at all, that the book's constant self-regeneration—prose giving birth to a poem, the poem inciting further prose—provides all the unity that Williams wanted. "Unity," he says in "An Essay on Virginia," is "the shallowest, the cheapest deception of all composition. In nothing is the banality of the intelligence more clearly manifested" (Imag., 321). But if "unity" is not important to Williams, "composition" is. His thinking on composition may have been influenced by the personal theology of Kandinsky, who wrote:

As examples of the new symphonic composition, in which the melodic element plays an infrequent and subordinate part, I have added reproductions of four of my own pictures.

They represent three different sources of inspiration:

(1) A direct impression of nature, expressed in purely pictorial form. This I call an "Impression."

(2) A largely unconscious, spontaneous expression of inner character, non-material nature. This I call an "Improvisation."

(3) An expression of a slowly formed inner feeling, tested and worked over repeatedly and almost pedantically. This I call a "Composition." Reason, consciousness, purpose, play an overwhelming part. But of calculation nothing appears: only feeling. . . .

I should like to remark finally that, in my opinion, we are fast approaching a time of reasoned and conscious composition, in which the painter will be proud to declare his work constructional—this in contrast to the claim of the impressionists that they could explain nothing, that their art came by inspiration.[15]

Williams is not willing to give up the concept of inspiration (for that matter, neither is Kandinsky, except as an excuse for inarticulateness)—too often Williams had felt the "fit" upon him: "I would be like a woman at term; no matter what else was up, that demand had to be met" (*Auto.*, "Foreword"). But he is always trying to explain his inspiration and, more important, to channel it into significant form.

Spring and All is Williams' first "symphonic" or "constructional" work of any length. Earlier, in *Al Que Quiere!* and *Sour Grapes*, he had pursued the liberating precepts of Imagism, with results analogous to Kandinsky's "impressions." *Kora in Hell* was a mind-opening experiment in the "largely unconscious, spontaneous expression of inner character" which Williams and Kandinsky both term "improvisation." *Spring and All* tries not to sacrifice any of the gains made in the earlier volumes. The objects it evokes are as fiercely particularized as any of the objects in Williams' "imagist" poems, and both the prose and poetry of the book are as associational and spontaneous as any improvisation. But *Spring and All* goes beyond the earlier works in its structural ambitions, its attempt to compose the warring factions of the poet's psyche into viable angles of combat from which productive rather than destructive tensions might be generated.

It is an ironic measure of Williams' success in this attempt that he produced very little poetry for years afterward. "Della Primavera Trasportata al Morale" and "The Descent of Winter," both written toward the end of the decade, are impressive works, but they would seem more so had they not been preceded by *Spring and All*. In fact, they do not add in any significant way to the innovations of that earlier work. In 1932, Williams wrote to Kay Boyle, "For myself, I have written little poetry recently. Form, the form has been lacking" (*SL*, 129). Unlike many poets once they have "found their voice," Williams refused to live off the capital of a "horde of skills," as he puts it. He would rather wait until he could make a genuine new beginning, as he did in fact do several times more in his life, most dramatically in the forties with his experiments in the "variable foot."

Williams had the humility and insight to see himself as a forerunner rather than as a summative genius who produces masterpieces. His function was to begin—incessantly—and to leave the completions to others. As a result, he is to many of today's poets what Whitman was to him: a father, a fellow conspirator, a rich source of liberating attitudes and techniques, an endless pleasure. In 1923, in *The Great American Novel*, Williams expresses his position in an idiom recalling Whitman's dismissal of "the classics": "What good to talk to me of Santayana and your later critics. I brush them aside. They do not apply. They do not reach me any more than a baby's hand reaches the moon. I am far under them. I am less, far less if you will. I am a beginner. I am an American" (*Imag.*, 175).

Afterword: A Prologue

Williams published *Spring and All* and his prose work, *The Great American Novel*, in Europe in 1923, the year in which he turned forty. The world received his sixth and seventh books as it had the five before them, in silence.

His feelings about America had always been ambivalent, and that ambivalence grew deeper as it became entangled with frustration. Reviewing an early book of stories by Kay Boyle, he began, "There is, in a democracy, a limit beyond which thought is not expected to leap. All men being presumed equal, it becomes an offense if this dead limit be exceeded" (*Imag.*, 338). Yet in 1923 and 1924 Williams was busy composing one of the most passionate and perceptive love letters America has ever received. Titled *In the American Grain*, it was brought out in a handsome edition in 1925 by Albert and Charles Boni. It was not the publishing event of the season.

No doubt the reception for such contrary works as Williams was writing would be uncertain at any time, but in 1923 and for several years thereafter the silence was intensified by the literary explosion that had preceded it, the publication in 1922 of T. S. Eliot's "The Waste Land." "It wiped out our world as if an atom bomb had been dropped upon it and our brave sallies into the unknown were turned to dust" (*Auto.*, 174).

The publication and public acclaim of a work of genius based on an aesthetic that is antithetical to one's own might understandably be discouraging. But Williams' reaction went beyond discouragement to despair; his confidence in his own approach to art was shaken by Eliot's triumph. Were the critics saying "willfully the wrong thing, or have we really been bluffed out of existence by our difficulties?" he asked Marianne Moore in 1923 (*SL*, 58). After *Spring and All*, eleven years passed before he published another volume of poetry. One reason was probably Eliot's success. Another may have been his own success, known to only a few, in *Spring and All*. For decades thereafter he could not outdo himself; some think he never did. His wife, Florence, said recently that *Spring and All* is still her favorite. Poets as different as W. S. Merwin and Louis Zukofsky have implied the same.

For these or other reasons he turned increasingly to prose, just as a dozen years earlier, in a different poetic bind, he had turned to plays. Some of these works, like the locally brilliant, intentionally formless *The Great American Novel* (1923), are experimental in a quasi-Joycean way; others seem (for Williams) fairly straightforward. In 1925, he published *In the American Grain*, a psychic prehistory of the United States; in 1928, *A Voyage to Pagany*, his first full novel; in 1929, *Last Nights of Paris*, a translation of Philippe Soupault's witty experimental novel; in 1932, *A Novelette and Other Prose*, more of his own experimental fiction and experimental criticism; and also in 1932, *The Knife of the Times*, his first collection of short stories. In all, six stylistically distinct, and for the most part distinguished, books of prose in a single decade.

Perhaps some day there will be an adequate critical ac-
counting for the explosion of prose activity during these years.
Such an appraisal will be complicated by the existence of
Williams' one failure in prose—a book called *The Embodiment of Knowledge*.[1] Written in spurts during 1928 and 1929,
and left unpublished until 1974, it is ostensibly a book on
education, a "presentation of a new theory of knowledge"
(75). The book is at once fascinating and extremely boring;
it is obsessed, repetitious, sloppy, occasionally profound, and
in places seems quite mad. Some of the ideas he expresses
are familiar from his other works, but the sentences which
contain them seem somehow wall-eyed, self-defeating. Frequently, the syntax will render an entire paragraph indeci-
pherable. At other points, the meaning will be clear but out-
landish: "We should employ professional readers, craftsmen
to take scientific and philosophic works and make of them
each in its turn as it appears ten words—which is all, if that
many, with which we can possibly be concerned" (93).

The formlessness of the work is apparently intentional. In
a scribbled note to himself on the title page, he proposes that
the numerous short chapters be arranged in no particular order. The book is to have no structural unity. Elsewhere he
gives what must suffice as a reason for this decision: "A literary essay is intended but in a manner unprecedented—not the
consecutive step by step logic but a single break through—as
of troops through a line of entrenchments—single but more
disordered (apparently) a much more disordered-appearing
progress—measured only by what we say—to the establishment
(of an advanced position) of work by this good—and make a
world for it" (96). The almost random use of parentheses and
dashes in this sentence typifies his approach throughout. It is
as if, having decided to free the book as a whole from the

"tyranny" of structural logic, Williams decided to go all the way and free the individual words from logical relationships to one another. The result, he writes, could be a "break through." In reality, it is a breakdown.

The reason may lie in a confusion over the purpose of the book. Ostensibly a lecture to Williams' two teenage sons about education, it is really a personal working through of ideas, conflicting self-images, and anxieties. That would be fair enough, but for the compulsive sabotage Williams works on his own reflections. The following is a revealing admission: "Afraid lest he be caught in a net of words, tripped up, bewildered and so defeated—thrown aside—a man hesitates to write down his innermost convictions. Especially is this true after forty when all his life is formed . . . into a single strand which allows him to say to himself that life is to him a reasonable thing. . . . If this be lost, this comforting inward sense of his own personal integrity lost in a crashing together of words . . . it is the end. He fears" (104). Yet his own endangered integrity pushes him on to probe the wound, to test his precarious convictions, "to strike straight to the core of his inner self, by words" (105).

The book is a hymn to wholeness, a wholeness he could not feel in his own divided psyche. Perhaps he hoped to spare his sons the agony at the center of his own life. But Williams seemed unable to attack the cause of that agony directly, and so his book heals no one, spares no one; he tortures himself through it, as he once wrote (to Marianne Moore) that he tortured himself through life. The desperate need to make himself clear, at least to himself, is exacerbated by the fear of being too explicit, as if to explain himself fully would be to explain himself away. In confusion, aesthetic or psychological, there is only futility; but without mystery, the gen-

erative paradox of unity within diversity, there is no energy
and thus no creation.

In the obsessive discussion of Shakespeare, the "whole"
man, versus Bacon, the walking encyclopedia, the reader is
meant to see a modern parallel with Williams (or the whole
man he wished to be) and Eliot, who knew much in his head
but apparently little with his "whole being." The indigestible
fact that in 1929 Williams was unknown and Eliot famous
had to be dealt with. What made it worse was the fact that
Williams himself was not writing much poetry and was certainly making no breakthroughs.

If he had been writing the "whole" poetry he wanted to
write, it is unlikely that this book would ever have come into
existence. Certainly, Williams was never close to insanity in
any clinical sense, although his writings are full of references
to it and flirtations with it. But *The Embodiment of Knowledge* shows Williams at a moment of great instability.[2] By
1929, the block keeping him from poetry was already breaking up, but he knew he still had no major work (as Crane
had, in "The Bridge") to hold up in opposition to "The
Waste Land." He feared he never would.

The publication of *Embodiment* can only help prolong the
current fashion to deride Williams' critical writings (among
which this work would have to be placed). Defense of
Williams' aesthetic theorizing has come mostly from other
poets, that is, from those who have personally benefited from
it. Among professional critics there seems almost a resent-
ment toward it. Hyatt H. Waggoner, in his massive *American Poets from the Puritans to the Present*,[3] expresses affection
for Williams' poetry, but vents his annoyance at those few
critics who, in their zeal to justify or perhaps just to

understand Williams' aesthetic theories, "pass over jumbled
and self-contradictory ideas as 'seeming paradoxes'" (371).
Like Yvor Winters and many others, he finds Williams a
muddy thinker, at times almost a fool. Waggoner's error is
pernicious because it is only half an error and may have a
long half-life in which to harm undergraduate minds. Williams readily admits that he lacks the learning of an Eliot or
a Pound and claims only to possess a "slow but accurate understanding." Williams has moments of bravado and occasional moments of spite, and like all of us he has his lapses
from clarity. But those lapses are far less frequent than is generally admitted.

Part of the problem for the critic is that Williams often
carries the methods of his poetry over into his discursive prose.
He may juxtapose "remote realities" without supplying the
common cement of logic to bind them together. Thus, an
essay about Juan Gris becomes an exercise in Cubistic collage
and reconstitution: "As the gates closed and the bridge slowly
swung open wasting his time—enforcing a stand-still, he
thought again of 'Juan Gris,' making a path through the ice.
That was the name of the approaching tug boat seen through
the branches of a bare beech tree. It had a white cabin and a
black stack with a broad yellow band around it" (*Imag.*, 284).
What could be clearer? There is no reader who will not at
once "see" what Williams means, even if he does not understand what he has seen. To talk about this passage at all, one
must take the same approach that one takes when talking
about his poetry. The enforced passivity, for instance, "wasting my time," could be related to the condition of passive
receptivity depicted in the opening of "The Right of Way":
"In passing with my mind / on nothing." As in the case of

good poetry, paraphrase here would lessen the effect, reduce the crisp sensory experience to a warm formula. Dr. Williams is willing to leave that to those who have patience for the job.

Waggoner asserts that "if ability to handle abstractions is taken as *the* mark of intelligence, then he was . . . very much less 'intelligent' than Stevens or Eliot or Pound, or perhaps than any modern poet with comparable fame and achievement" (371). The meaning of the quotation marks around "intelligent" is not clear. Either Waggoner is at the last moment holding himself back from declaring flatly that Williams was dense, or he is suggesting that there may be another sort of intelligence than the kind that juggles abstractions—in which case the "ability to handle abstractions" is not *the* mark of intelligence after all.

Apparently the second possibility is the correct one, for a few pages later Waggoner says that Williams is at his best "when he writes from his deeper mind and not from his efforts at thinking" (383). Again pernicious. At least the statement allows Williams a "deeper mind," but whether "deeper" means "more profound" or merely "less rational" is again not clear. Could Waggoner be thinking of Wordsworth's spontaneous overflow of powerful emotions? But has there ever been a completely successful poem, even by Wordsworth, that did not contain that "overflow" within some adequate form, fashioned by verbal technique after considerable "efforts at thinking"? And on the other hand, has there been a single great poet since the eighteenth century who did not desire to break through the glib logic of his conscious mind into a "deeper mind"? The statement is simply without meaning.

It should be said, Mr. Waggoner is a good critic, except here. So is Randall Jarrell, except where he says that Williams "is even less logical than the average good poet—he is an 'intellectual' in neither the good nor the bad sense of the word."[4] Yvor Winters is a good critic, too. So are they all.

Williams is quite aware of the problems his work poses for the reader and in *Spring and All* offers this assurance: "There is no confusion—only difficulties" (*Imag.*, 140). Sometimes it's hard to differentiate confusion and difficulties, and it is perhaps natural for critics, reading what appears to be a straightforward essay on Matisse or on poetics or on the state of Virginia, to assume confusion in an author who will not provide them with logical, discursive prose.

In his critical prose, Williams does indulge in some logical contradictions, but for Waggoner to spend approximately half of his essay exposing them is to greatly exaggerate their importance. D. H. Lawrence's criticism also harbors contradictions, and he is still a great critic, a generative critic who incites other minds to creative acts of their own. Williams' criticism is in the same class.

Perceptively, Waggoner writes that Williams' mother and Ezra Pound (or what they represented) were the "two paramount influences on Williams as a poet[;] and the two influences, working at different levels of consciousness, pulled him in different directions" (373). But he assigns Pound's influence to a superficial level of consciousness, to Williams' "consciously held [that is, wrong] ideas about poetry" (374), whereas his mother's influence "shaped the man" (374), presumably on the level of the "deeper mind." The contradictions in Williams' statements about poetry can be assigned to "confusion" only by a critic who fails to see that the significance of Pound—the shaper, the "father," the manipulating intellect—was just as deep as that of the mother. If, as I have argued, the contradictions in Williams' writing proceed from psychic antagonisms so fundamental as to approach the realm of archetype, it seems unfair and a little foolish to accuse Williams of being unable to handle abstractions or to maintain a seemly veneer of logic.

A final point: by concluding that Williams wrote "better than he knew," Mr. Waggoner is again stepping into tall grass. Every writer secretly hopes that his words will somehow, at least occasionally, transcend his personal limitations. In the previous chapter it was suggested that this blessing alighted upon Williams in some of the poems of *Spring and All*. But writing better than one knows is hardly the same as not knowing what one is about. The notion that Williams is merely an instinctive writer—a sort of modern primitive—cannot survive a careful reading of the poems he wrote. It will certainly not survive a reading of the chapter, "Syntax in Rutherford," in Hugh Kenner's altogether remarkable book, *The Pound Era*.[5]

For Williams, the years from 1924 to 1929, to judge from the tone of the works produced, were a time of reexamination and transition similar in intensity to the period between 1913 and 1918. Williams was in his forties, a transitional time in many men's lives, when youth is no longer available as an excuse or as a resource. In 1927, he took Florence and the boys to Switzerland and left them there. His marriage with her was still solid but perhaps in need of ventilation, if one may judge by their mutual decision to separate for that nine-month period. No doubt another reason for the separation was that he felt that a year's schooling in Europe would do the boys good.

Sailing home by himself aboard the SS *Pennland*, Williams immediately felt a renewal of creative energy and a great surge of love for his wife. He wrote letter after letter to her from on board ship (*SL*, 71–91) expressing a sort of frightened happiness: "I was thinking that we are doing just what we want to do. . . . The risks had to be faced or we should all have been less than we are. . . . The thing is that we have ended a period as you say and now we are going on" (*SL*, 75).

This decisive separation seems to have been immediately beneficial, for he found himself able once again to write poetry. "I have written constantly on this trip," he says in another shipboard letter, "that is, as I write, in mad spurts. . . . I have decided on the title and general contents of a book, my next book of poems and written the first two poems which I'll send also later. The title is *Sacred and Profane*. They are to be all love poems" (*SL*, 85).

The eventual result, twenty-one poems and eighteen prose pieces called "The Descent of Winter," was never published as a book in itself. Ezra Pound gave forty pages of his magazine *The Exile* to it (Autumn, 1928). In 1970, in the collection *Imaginations*, the work again became available in its ragged entirety. During the forty-two-year interim, no one but Louis Zukofsky seemed to miss it.

Although the work bears a physical similarity to *Spring and All*, particularly in its alternation of prose and poetry, it has none of the structural ambitions and not enough of the excitement of the earlier work. Its primary value seems to be that it got Williams back to writing poetry. An early version of "The Descent of Winter," a ninety-six-page manuscript at present in the Lockwood Library, contains several pages that indicate what the original plan may have been. Here is one of the pages:

SACRED AND PROFANE   (SCORIA)

1.

nothing less
    than perfect
      would I be for you

          every moment day
and night
        seeing or dreaming

    the world
    through your eyes

---

    she reached to the top
shelf for soap
        for me

    so that her taught [*sic*]
        white thighs grew bare
above
      the wrinkled
    garters

and I who spend my life
      more or less among
        these things

    My heart fluttered

    like an angel's

At the bottom of the page he added: "Note: THE ANGEL'S
SERENADE . . . simple contrast of mood – tempo, meter
(You:She.) Each under a *single* title. Scoria."

    The line separating the upper ("sacred") and lower ("pro-
fane") halves of the poem reminds one of similarly visible distinctions in *Kora in Hell* between the cultured and the chthonic
voices. That the "profane" section of the poem should end

with a reference to angels suggests the circular nature of the feelings that surround the diametrical distinction. Williams' poem, like his life, is "broken, yet woven together."[6] Like many other lyrics of this period, it looks back at techniques already developed. But there is an original twist to this version of the old dichotomy, and something suggestive of the future in the arrangement of the lines. It would not be hard to re-arrange the poem into three-step lines such as those he used obsessively in his later works.

Only a few of the poems that Williams allowed into the final version of "The Descent of Winter" exhibit anything like this "simple contrast of mood – tempo, meter." Perhaps the lyric that comes closest is the entry dated "10/21." In the first stanza, this poem describes horizontal windblown flames in a rubbish heap; in the second, the sufferings of old people. Again one is reminded of earlier works characterized by a shifting of category, a yoking together of remote realities which only the imagination can bridge.

One's enjoyment of the fine lyrics in the final version of "Descent" is compromised by one's annoyance at the baf-fling and unnecessary obscurities. One example of obscurity is this two-line poem, dated "10/13":

> a beard . . . not of stone but particular
> hairs purpleblack . . . lies upon his stale breast
>
> [*Imag.*, 237]

It represents a radical abridgement of a torrential two-page prose improvisation called "Hairy Face," in which little girls grow into full-breasted women "figged full of seeds," and leaves from innumerable trees rush to the ground ("they fall, see that, they fall ~~like~~ a beard . . . impossible to count them rake them up"). What is a reader who is not privy to manuscript collections to do with the two-line "poem" Williams has given him? It is not fair.

The above entry is not an isolated example of this self-defeating lack of consideration on the poet's part. In the final version of "Descent," the short prose entry "Travelling in Fast Company" has been snipped out of a seven-page improvisation of the same title. The most imaginative reader would be helpless to explain the fragmented sentence "Its hands stuck up in the air like prongs," in the middle of a paragraph on motorcyclists. On the fourth manuscript page of the improvisation, the needed context will be discovered:

[The sick infant's] hands have all the markings in the palms. . . . Life line says it will live to be six hundred and fifty. . . . Lies there blinking. Its lips working. Moves its head corkscrew wise. Probably sick of lying on the back of its occiput and doesn't know how to change the position or can't. Its hands stuck up in the air like prongs. Just sticking up in the air, fingers spread apart.

For various reasons, then, "The Descent of Winter" must be considered as at best a qualified success.[7] Williams made only one other major poetic effort before the end of the twenties, a piece called "Della Primavera Trasportata Al Morale." A version of it was printed in the 1930 *Imagist Anthology*, and another version exists in manuscript (L). On the title page of this latter version, Williams wrote and then crossed out the words, "Preceded by an introduction: THE DESCENT OF WINTER." One is tempted to infer from these words that Williams perceived the aesthetic self-sufficiency of the later piece and the incompleteness of the earlier one. Not that "Primavera" is free of intentional and perhaps insoluble puzzles. The most immediate problem is to determine how long the work really is. Is it the eight-page section (*CEP,*

57–64) called "Della Primavera Trasportata Al Morale," or
is it the whole twenty-five-page block (*CEP*, 57–81) collectively titled "Della Primavera Transportata [*sic*] Al Morale"?
And is the difference in spelling intentional, a method of distinguishing between a part and the whole (or between a single poem and a "suite" of poems)? Critics differ and seem not
to notice one another's differences. I am inclined to see a suite
of poems, but recognize at the same time Williams' playful
conspiracy to thwart easy classification.

The spirit of play is at the heart of the work and contributes to its great appeal. One of the techniques of delight has
to do with the briskness of the pace. In the first poem ("Trasportata") especially, the eye trapezes from line to line in order to keep up with short swinging rhythms infectious with
energy. As in certain earlier poems ("Primrose," "The Cold
Night"), there are excited repetitions of key words, leaving
one with the irreverent but not altogether irreligious feeling
that one is listening to a liturgy recorded at 33 rpm and played
at 45:

> Moral
>> the redhead sat
>> in bed with her legs
>> crossed and talked
>> rough stuff
>
> Moral
>> the door is open
>
> Moral
>> the tree moving diversely
>> in all parts   [*CEP*, 60]

Excerpts do not do justice to the movement of the poem as
a whole. That overall movement is perhaps best described by

the last two lines above: "the [poem] moving diversely / in all parts," continually tossed by contrary spring winds. The feeling is quite different from the grand pendulum swings of, for example, a sonnet. Williams' poem provides a remarkable new music, "having the form / of motion," as he puts it in another poem in this same group.

The manuscript version suggests, although it does not prove, that almost all the poems in the suite were written in a remarkably short period of time—perhaps only a week. The entries in "The Descent of Winter," written the previous fall, took three months to write. The greater speed of composition and the greater artistic success of "Primavera" may be simply coincidental, or they may suggest that Williams' mind had at last regained that fluid condition of which he has spoken so often, a condition which made possible a "new sweep of imagination" (*SL*, 97).

Besides the long title poem, the "Primavera" group includes such remarkable successes as "The Sea Elephant" and "The Botticellian Trees." The manuscript shows signs of important revisions but not of drastic ones. Earlier versions, of course, may turn up to contradict any deductions one makes, but present evidence suggests that the Lockwood Manuscript represents something close to the first state of the poems. If so, Williams was indeed writing with a firm hand. The final revisions (as reflected in the published versions) are for the most part confined to excisions, the rearrangement of lines, and occasional substitutions (usually of a highly specific word for a more general one). In "The Botticellian Trees," for example, the lines "until the strict / sentences" are revised to "until the stript / sentences," in order better to anticipate the highly sensual image that follows: "move as a woman's / limbs

under cloth." Also in that poem, the final version contains a
line composed solely of an ellipsis:

> the smiles of love—
>
> . . . . . .

The reader is expected to pause, perhaps to dwell a moment
on the smiles of love, but surely not to try to guess what
words may have been left out. The manuscript version sup-
plies the (wisely) extracted lines:

> the smiles of love
> which though it lives
>
> in seclusion and prays
> things of gentler
>
> letters

The stitches left in the poem after the operation to remove
these lines represent the only visible flaw in the poem's deli-
cate physics.

Although the poems in the "Primavera" group all have a
fresh, newborn quality about them, they reiterate themes
found in Williams' poetry from the beginning. Even the
somewhat obscure title "The Botticellian Trees" has its origin
in Williams' earliest writings (see Appendix B, "Vegetation
in yard, Obser. concern."). It is as if Williams were writing
only one poem all his life, the same long nature poem (which
to him meant love poem)—from the first sonnet about skunk
cabbage to the last great elegy, "Asphodel, That Greeny
Flower."

A solid line of work pursued resolutely is at last seen as a
curve, even as a circle, precluding loss. Williams' distrust of
the merely linear expressed itself in everything he did. One

suspects its presence even in the way in which he chose to
arrange his poems for the 1951 *Collected Earlier Poems*. Before Emily Mitchell Wallace's extraordinary bibliography
appeared in 1968, critics despaired of straightening out the
chronology of Williams' early work. Since 1968, they have
merely muttered about his carelessness or his eccentricity.
But it seems likely that, in choosing to scramble the order of
his poems, Williams was expressing in yet a new form a characteristic psychic duality: he was trying to make himself
available to understanding, vulnerable to the gaze of all eyes,
friendly or hostile, in a Whitmanesque self-exposure to "my
townspeople"; and at the same time he was trying to prevent
too easy an understanding, to mislead all but the most reso-
lute, and through a "judicious involvement of the meaning"
to make damn fools of as many critics as he could.

Another reason can be deduced from the short lyric "Descent" printed near the end of *The Collected Earlier Poems*
and never published elsewhere:

> From disorder (a chaos)
> order grows
> —grows fruitful.
> The chaos feeds it. Chaos
> feeds the tree.   [*CEP*, 460]

Perhaps Williams felt that by making a chaos of his early
(and not-so-early) poetry, he was creating a new, nonlinear
order, even in a sense a poem, "seeking to be realized" (*Auto.*,
362). If so, there is added meaning to the inscription he wrote
in his wife's copy: "decipher it as you may—and best luck."

In addition, of course, the words "chaos" and "order" bring
to mind all the inner dichotomies of which we have been
speaking in this book. The word "tree" is another reminder.
From the sickly, blossom-encrusted branch he spoke of in a

fifth-grade composition to the locust tree seen outside a window at the end of *Paterson*, trees have been the subject of Williams' deepest reveries throughout his life. Here, indeed, one may speak of the "deeper mind," the faculty of making profound connections. Trees begin to flower, the flower becomes a poem, the poem is a dance, the dancer is a woman, the woman is in the man, the man is a poet, the poem becomes a tree. Williams feared that his compulsion to "crash all together" might be a symptom of madness, but he also suspected that his ability to perceive the cohesiveness of the extraneous, and his reckless willingness to express those perceptions at whatever price, might constitute his "only value" (*SL*, 98). For Williams, the imaginative breaking apart and rewelding of the world around him was, like breathing, a continual process, making everything he wrote a prologue to everything else, regardless of chronology.

Williams emerges as a crucial figure in American literature because he managed to escape whole from the great industrial desert in which most men live unroused, disconnected. He is revered by younger poets, not because he discovered the so-called variable foot, but because he showed them that the closer one stays to the ground—in direct touch with one's feelings and one's physical perceptions—the closer one grows to the healing world of imagination, in which all the old myths, stripped of their outworn names, begin to move again and make miraculous sense.

Appendix A

The following poems are from the Yale American Literature Collection, Beinecke Library. The originals, seven typed pages, may be found at the front of a folder of correspondence with Viola Jordan. Since "Pastoral 1" was published (in different form) in *Others* in 1915, it seems likely that all the poems were written at about that time.

PASTORALS and SELF-PORTRAITS.

Self-Portrait 1.

You lie packed,
Dark:
Turned sluggishly
By plough.
Wheels stir you –
   Up behind them!
You tissue out
You drink light
And go in clouds!

Pastoral 1.

The old man who goes about
Gathering dog lime
Walks in the gutter

Without looking up
And his tread
Is more majestic than
That of the Episcopal minister
Approaching the pulpit
Of a Sunday.
Meanwhile
The little sparrows
Hop ingenuously
About the pavement
Quarreling
Over those things
That interest them
With sharp voices
But we who are wiser
Shut ourselves in
On either hand
And no one knows
Whether we think good
Or evil.
                              These things
Astonish me beyond words!

Idyl

Wine of the grey sky
Wine of happiness
Invisible rain
Driven down
You bathe me
And I am refreshed:

Yesterday
I was in the city
I stood before
The new station
Watching

The white clouds
Passing
The great Hermes
And flying,
Flying toward Greece.
I saw
The fluted columns
(Not ground
  Piece into piece
  But fitted with plaster)
I saw the frieze
Of acanthus :
All that has endured
Through the long days
And the long, long nights
And I thought
Of Phidias ,
O wine of the grey sky ,
Watching
As there passed
Clouds
White and formless
Without word
Without sign
Above his Parthanon
Out toward India
And the sea!

Seraph

I was here alone,
The lamp back of me
There under the beams –
The heat of the fire in my face.
I straightened and turned

There stood you!
Immobile,

Gleaming with light!
The miraculous vision
Flaming, flashing itself
Upon me, an acid
To quench thirst
Once for all.

That is why when
You came forward
With your excuses
Asking if you had
Frightened me
I seized you,
Held you eagerly in my arms

But it was gone.

Pastoral 2.

If I talk to things
Do not flatter yourself
That I am mad
Rather realize yourself
To be deaf and that
Of two evils, the plants
Being deaf likewise,
I choose that
Which proves by other
Attributes worthier
Of the distinction.

Hear me
You who listen without malice.
Hear me
You crusts of blue moss,
And black earth
In the twisted roots
Of the white tree!

Hear me, black trees
The wind
Howling in your branches!
Hear me
Long red-grass
Matted down
And standing in the wind!
Hear me
Driven leaves!
Hear me
Though you never tell
The cause of this terror
That strikes me back
Feverishly upon petty business:
Saving the sick,
Getting shelter, food
And delights for my dear family –
I long
To fling aside clothes
And crawl in naked
There among you
Cold as it is!

Hear me
For I am wise,
Wiser than you –
Though you have virtues
Greater than mine.
I will give you
A counsel for it further on
When I have said my fill.
  – wiser than you
Though you have virtues
Greater than mine:
You do not drive yourselves,
It is the wind's knives
That battle at you

From the outside –
You do not generate
Your own poisons.

See!
(Take note of this
You who have eyes.)
See these futile colors
That keep me from the wind.

Do not think
It is fear of these
That holds me
From *you* likewise—
I would fling them by in a moment
And the roof menders there,
Peacefully hammering,
Would rush down
And carry me away –
Even so it would be
A wise thing to have done
Were it not
That this hide
I have drawn about myself
To shield me
Has bound me more subtly
Than you have imagined.

It is no good
To strip the bark
From the old tree
It will not be young again –
I have bound myself
Better than that!

Kiss the wind when it kills you
Lean your surfaces
Against the frost
With your whole heart –

You have taken the counsel
Before given.

Self-Portrait 2.

It is raining.
Fall!
You whitelivered kill-joys
Fall!
You heavy bellied sluts,
Fall from the sky!
Fall onto the edged leaves,
Let the bayonettes of the grass
Receive you –
Drive you to the ground:
There be broken finally
 – and your life ends!

As for me – ?
Beat upon my head
And upon my shoulders
You frighten me but little.
Let your very eyes pop out
Against the feather I wear
And dance down the edge
Of my sombrero – !
I'll keep my way in spite of all.

Only the flowers
Are kind to them –
Lips opening upward.

Idyl

They say to me, "There is
A roaring god outside
Beating the trees!"
I go hurriedly
And find

thunderstorm

Two unfortunates
Cowering in the wind.
I think of this
As I lie here, warm
Watching the blinding white
That was saffron
Change to steel blue
Behind shaking trees.

I raise my head and
Sight leaps twenty miles
To the bleak horizon,
"But my desires,"
I say to myself
"Are thirty years
Behind all this."

It is late.
My wife comes out
And tucks me in
Telling me
Not to hurry –
 – Not to hurry!
She brings our baby
And puts him
In the bed beside me.
I move over
Into the cold sheets
To make room for him
And thinking
Of the freezing poor
I consider myself
Happy –
Then we kiss.

Grotesque

The city has tits in rows.
The country is in the main – male,

It buts me with blunt stub-horns,
Forces me to oppose it
Or be trampled.

The city is full of milk
And lies still for the most part.
These crack skulls
And spill brains
Against her stomach.

Appendix B

The following are selections from a file marked "GENERAL INDEX," which Williams kept active between 1908 and 1911. A discussion of this file and its meaning will be found in Chapter One. I have confined the contents of this Appendix to items not discussed in that chapter. In the hope of aiding scholarship, I have listed almost everything Williams wrote about his reading habits at the time. As a consequence it has been necessary to scant his interminable and sometimes fascinating lists of birds, trees, and flowers seen around Rutherford.

Books to read and buy

Moeurs Intimes du Passé
Allg. path & diag. der Rind T.B.   1 Hamburger Viers. 3.30
Mode der 18th cent.   Max v. Boem.
Weinachtsbackerei
Wilhelm Meister = Goethe
Frau Sorge – Sudermann
Discover of Am. in 5th cent. B.C. by Chinese priests
Toscanelli a Fernan Mortina et Col d'apres Vignaud Rouen '02
Macaulay's Machiavelli
Dichtung ŭ Wahrheit – Goethe . . .

New England Idyls.   Miss Wilkins . . .
Old Creole days   G. Cabel
Biglow Papers – Lowell
Plays of Aristophenes   John Hookman Frere
Display of Heraldry, Gwillim
Foundations of Rhetoric   Prof. Hill., A.S.
          (chapt. common misuse of conjuncts.)
English Prose – Earle
Wendell English Composition
English Grammar Past & Present
          J. E. Nesfield (list of preps. fol. verbs.)
Talk & Talkers – Stephenson
Isochromatische Tafel – Dr. Stilling
Chinese Ghosts – Lafcadio Hearn
Impressions de theater   Juleo Le Maître
Une page d'Amour   Emil Jola
(Descriptions of Paris from Trocadero.)
Laocoön – Lessing (Iliad.)
Chapman's Homer
Journal of the plague year. De Foe
The Art of Fiction – Henry James
The persons in the tale – Stevenson
Autobiography – Anthony Trollop
Technical elements of style in literature   Stevenson
Bier Treatment (hyperaemia) . . .
German Medical dictionary
Fitzboodle & yellow plush papers
Thackery
System Der Dr. Techn.
Die Deutsche Clinic

Books to read

Bronte, Emily
          Wuthering heighths
          Poems

Books read

Origin of Species	fin. May 3– 08
Tempest–Shakes.	fin. May 4–
Frau Sorge–	" Jan. –'10
Measure for M.	" June –'10
Schillers plays. *12.*	" Nov. –'09

Books to be read

La Fontaine et ses fables.   H. Taine
Hist. of St. Louis – Joinville
Marbot – Napoleonic wars
(Books ment. in Mathews "Theater")
Tisch-Reden   Luther
Anthropology
Descent of man.   Darwin
Prolongation of life.   Metchnikoff
Harmony   Jadassohn
Composition   "
Counterpoint   "
Fractures   Stirnson
Pioneers of France in t' New World   Francis Parkman
The Jesuits in N. Am'ca   "   "
La Salle & discovery of G't west   "   "
The old regime in Canada under L XIV   "   "
Count Fronteric & Meut. under L XIV   "   "
      (Little, Brown & Co – Boston 1900)
Buccaneers & Pirates of our coasts   Stockton
History of America   Parkman
Pagent of Women   Lucas

Books by E. V. Lucas.

      The MacMillan Company   64 – 5th Ave.

Mr. Ingleside
Orer Bemerton's
Listener's Lore

The Gentlest Art
The Second Post
The Ladies Pagent
Some Friends of Mine
   Travel
A Wanderer in London
" " " Holland
" " " Paris

Books etc. to be read

Holt's diseases of childhood
Hirst's obstetrics.
    psychology
Metchinikoffs 3 books
Some books on Harmony
     Composition
     Counterpoint
Autobiography – Phin. Barnum
Benvenuto Cellini
Temple Ed. Dante – 6 vol. Dent
Paget Toynbee life of Dante . . .
Lionel Johnson – Earnest Dowson
Yeates – Mathiews– Bullen
The temple primers – Dante
  by Edmund G. Gardner M.A.
Longinus – on the Sublime
Aristotle – Poetics
Dante – De Vulgari Eloquio
Early Italian poets D. G. Rosetti
Institutional Hist. of Virginia in 17th cent.
P. H. Bruce LL.D. 2 vols G. P. Putnam's Sons
Champion II vol.
Francois Villon et son temp

Play. The Two Doctor Franks.

Man & wife both Drs. in same house.
He kind careful, too humble.

She masterful, wins   tries to convince him.   He sees &
gives in.
She carries it on.
Gets his patients, they divide.

Play.   Phoenix Juvenis

I   The house over the Passaic   people leave the others (Italians
come in.) are con[s]cious of degradation but She the child who
plays in the window Sundays in despight of the horrid.   The
murder by father.
A Greek mother.   but she dreams on.   Bellville quarry.

The ruin of me is the building[?] material of mother.

Poetry Form

Centrality of address, with vigor of purpose and enthusiastic conviction: to God, to my lady, to my brother, my friend my fellow
creature.

Poetry Form

Emotion does not continuously pertain except in the briefest ode.
When it does let it mould its form, for it is hot and can   but the
colder subject of less passion should hold or revert to the regular
form to which it is fit.
   No departure except the impossibility for passion to be contained which rarely occurs.

Poetry   The artists life.

It is simplification lives deeper as accord c̄ the generalities which
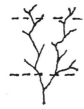 include the specialties which are elaboration
The growth & human change go on at these
places but he is deeper to the root   & ∴ has
no common commodity & exchange & barely
lives. ∴ must concentrate & support self purely
economic reasons.

Birds observed, wild in & about R.fd.

May 4 – [1908]   Pair of cat birds. P[assaic] River woods
May 4 –   Pair of blue jays flying about house
May 6 –   Male house wren singing in back yard. Perched
                 several times on hollow branch placed on out
                 house.
May 6 –   Robin nest in cherry tree nearing completion.
                 Chipping Sparrows nest nearing completion.
May 9 –   Along river. Pair of Baltimore orioles in mag-
                 nificent plumage. Both birds sang beautifully.
                 Also a harsh warning note.
                 Kingfisher flying over river.
May 9 –   Two yellow warblers.
May 9 –   The wrens changed houses and are now build-
                 ing in the house over door of shop.
May 10 –   Screech owl in edge of Kipp's woods. Chased
                 me, darting at my head and making two click-
                 ing sounds each time. Once it made a sound
                 between neigh of a horse and squeak of a
                 rat.   10 P.M.

Vegetation in yard, Obser. concern.

May 8   [1908] Mulberry tree not yet in full leaf. Certainly a
                 dainty light tree. Reminds me of Boticceli.
                 Lilacs in all but full bloom.
May 9   Planted 6 eggplants.
  "   "   "   small white birch tree which found in
                 street uprooted.
May 10   Beets, cress & second plant. of radishes above
                 ground. . . .
May 18   Quince blossoms falling.
                 Dogwood still in bloom.
May 20   Dogwood & Quince and lilacs all wilting rap-
                 idly. Columbines blue and purple in bloom.
May 22   Lillies of valley still in bloom.

May 23   Second planting of beans up.
                  "   "   " corn ".
              Poppies, cosmos up.
              Columbines pink and white w bloom.
May 28   Sweet Williams just starting to bloom.

References

Introduction

1. In an installment of *The H. D. Book* appearing in *A Caterpillar Anthology* (ed. Clayton Eshleman [New York: Doubleday, 1971], p. 67), Robert Duncan notes this same duality in Williams' thought and seems not at all distressed by it: "In the major phase of his last years, William Carlos Williams, the poet who was to have 'no ideas but in things,' would relate poetry to dream and to phantasy, as H. D. would in *Good Friend*."

CHAPTER ONE: Early Years, 1900–1909

1. Only a few of the letters written before 1910 appear in the *Selected Letters*. The bulk of them are in a vault in the Lockwood Memorial Library at Buffalo.

2. Oddly, in the *Autobiography* (53), Williams speaks of twenty-three volumes of free verse, not eighteen. There is no discoverable reason for this discrepancy.

3. Undated, unpublished letter, YALC.

4. K. L. Goodwin, *The Influence of Ezra Pound* (London: Oxford University Press, 1966), p. 2.

5. The page is reproduced in facsimile in *William Carlos Williams*, edited by Charles Abbott (Rutherford, N.J.: Fairleigh Dickinson University Press, 1974).

6. Her talk is included *ibid.*, pp. 20–30.

7. James E. Breslin, *William Carlos Williams, An American Artist*, New York: Oxford University Press, 1970.

8. Louise Bogan, *Achievement in American Poetry* (Chicago: Regnery, 1951), p. 3.

9. John Millington Synge, *Poems and Translations* (Dublin, 1911), pp. 3–4.

10. John Keats, *Poetical Works and Other Writings* (New York: Scribners, 1939), 2:11.

11. It is possible that one of the attractions of Keats was the fact that he formulated for Williams psychic prototypes of the conflicts that were raging inside him and which seemed too deep to be solved except symbolically.

12. Bliss Perry, *Walt Whitman, His Life and Work* (Boston: Houghton Mifflin, 1906), p. 74.

13. On a recently discovered Christmas shopping list from 1908, Williams lists, besides such items as a plaster bust of Voltaire, table mats, and Amiel's *Journal*, "Sonnets to months as decorated by Ed." Apparently, he considered these poems sufficiently autonomous to be extracted from the book without harm, and sufficiently conventional and inoffensive to be presented to a member of his family—perhaps to his mother—at Christmas.

14. Breslin relates the loneliness of the poet to the Romantic tradition: "Plainly, the melancholy author of this volume [*Poems*] is not an ordinary mortal, but one whose vision of the ideal makes him A Man Set Apart" (*William Carlos Williams, An American Artist*, p. 11). He also reminds us that Pound's work during this period, and even Eliot's, is imbued with "the melancholy of the outcast" (p. 13).

15. Vivienne Koch, *William Carlos Williams*, Norfolk, Conn.: New Directions, 1950.

16. In the spring of 1971, Mrs. Williams was approached by a scholar who wanted her permission to publish "Sauerkraut to the Cultured." Presumably, therefore, the play still exists, though Mrs. Williams does not know where it might be.

CHAPTER TWO: Transition Years, 1910–1917

1. Research by Mike Weaver confirms the general accuracy of the autobiographical references in *The Build-Up*. See his book, *William Carlos Williams, The American Background* (New York: Cambridge University Press, 1971), chs. 1 and 2.

2. Breslin, *William Carlos Williams, An American Artist*, p. 13.

3. Bram Dijkstra, *The Hieroglyphics of a New Speech: Cubism, Stieglitz, and the Early Poetry of William Carlos Williams*, Princeton: Princeton University Press, 1969.

4. For a more comprehensive list of Stieglitz' remarkable activities,

see the Appendix to *America and Alfred Stieglitz*, ed. Waldo Frank and others, New York: The Literary Guild, 1934.

5. From "On First Opening *The Lyric Year*." Reprinted in *New Directions 16* (1957), p. 9.

6. "La Flor," reprinted *ibid.*, pp. 10–11.

7. Ezra Pound, *The Selected Letters of Ezra Pound, 1907–1941*, ed. D. D. Paige (new ed., New York: New Directions, 1971), p. 28.

8. Reprinted in *New Directions 16* (1957), p. 13.

9. Interview conducted by Sidney Fields in the New York *Sunday Mirror*, June 18, 1950.

10. Alfred Kreymborg, *Troubadour, An Autobiography* (New York: Boni and Liveright, 1925), pp. 242–243.

11. James Guimond, in *The Art of William Carlos Williams: A Discovery and Possession of America* (Urbana, Ill.: University of Illinois Press, 1968), speaks of Williams' vulnerability, not only to people, but also to the industrial environment in which he lives: "The artist must first expose himself to his immediate world and *then* hope that it will not destroy him or his art" (p. 21).

12. These remarks by J. B. Kerfoot were prominently displayed at the front of the November 1915 issue of *Others*.

13. Linda Welshimer Wagner, *The Poems of William Carlos Williams: A Critical Study* (Middletown, Conn.: Wesleyan University Press, 1964), p. 22.

14. Pound, *Selected Letters*, p. 48.

15. Guimond, *The Art of William Carlos Williams*, pp. 26–27.

16. All letters to Brown quoted here and on succeeding pages are from an uncatalogued box in the Beinecke Library at Yale.

17. The epigraph to *Al Que Quiere!* comes from the story "The Man Who Resembled a Horse," which Williams and his father translated jointly and published in *The Little Review*, 5 (Dec. 1918), 42–53. Here is their rendition of the passage: "I had been an adventurous shrub which prolongs its filiments until it finds the necessary humus in new earth. And how I fed! I fed with the joy of tremulous leaves of chlorafile that spread themselves to the sun; with the joy with which a root encounters a decomposing corpse; with the joy with which convalescents take their vacillating steps in the light-flooded mornings of spring. . . ." In his third book, Williams saw himself as the iconoclastic spirit of paganism regaining its strength in a new land—an interesting contrast to Eliot, who in "The Waste Land" suggests the prototype of the tired, convalescent Christian.

18. *Leaves of Grass* (New York: Columbia University Press for the Facsimile Text Society, 1939), p. 15.

CHAPTER THREE: *Kora in Hell: Improvisations*

1. The abruptness of tone may be due in part to Williams' awareness of how slow Brown could be in bringing a book out, in part to Williams' tenseness over his father's condition. William G. Williams died on Christmas Day, 1918, a week after this letter was written.

2. Dijkstra, pp. 72–76, is particularly acute on this aspect of *Kora*.

3. Joseph Evans Slate, in his article, "Kora in Opacity: Williams' *Improvisations*" (*Journal of Modern Literature*, 1 [May 1971], 467), describes the difference this way: "The italicized notes have much longer sentences, fewer verbless phrases and exclamations, and always use formal rather than colloquial verb forms. There are no commands or questions in the italics, only declarative statements; and the italic statements often begin with long introductory clauses." So far so good. Unfortunately, Mr. Slate goes on to indulge a critical surmise: "By shifting styles between improvisations, Williams plays with the readers' expectations: the perception of a stylistic change coerces the mind into thinking that a genuine shift of approach has been made; because this has in fact not been done, the reader is finally forced to see the resemblances between the italics and the improvisations."

4. See, for instance, "The Use of Force" (*FD*, pp. 131–135).

5. Unpublished letter of June 10, 1921.

6. Quoted by Gaston Bachelard in *The Poetics of Reverie*, trans. Daniel Russell (New York: The Orion Press, 1969), p. 1.

7. See Auerbach's essay, "Odysseus' Scar," in *Mimesis: The Representation of Reality in Western Literature*, trans. Willard Trask (Princeton, New Jersey: Princeton University Press), chap. 1.

8. Rainer Maria Rilke, *Gesammelte Gedichte* (Frankfurt am Main: Insel, 1962), p. 488.

9. "The time of *Kora* precedes time," writes Joseph N. Riddel, attempting to characterize this tantalizing aspect of the book; "these are improvisations which progress neither rhetorically nor dialectically, but move like counterpoint in a temporal relation that denies linear time." "The Wanderer and the Dance: William Carlos Williams' Early Poetics," in *The Shaken Realist: Essays in Modern Literature in Honor of Frederick J. Hoffman*, ed. Melvin J. Friedman and John B.

Vickery (Baton Rouge, La.: Louisiana State University Press, 1970), p. 61.

10. René Taupin, *L'Influence du symbolisme français sur la poésie américaine*, Paris: Campion, 1929.

11. Ezra Pound, *Polite Essays* (London, Faber and Faber, 1937), p. 74.

12. "A Sketchbook of the Artist in His Thirty-Fourth Year: William Carlos Williams' *Kora in Hell: Improvisations*," in Friedman and Vickery, *The Shaken Realist*, p. 30.

13. Donald Sutherland, *Gertrude Stein, A Biography of Her Work* (New Haven, Conn.: Yale University Press, 1951), p. 133.

14. July 1919, p. 30.

15. Bachelard, *The Poetics of Reverie*, pp. 51–52.

16. Unpublished letter, January 6, 1911. Mike Weaver's comment, that here "Williams showed himself aware of the possibilities of inversion," seems to miss the point quite completely. *William Carlos Williams, The American Background*, p. 22.

17. Bachelard, *The Poetics of Reverie*, p. 49.

18. Bachelard, *The Poetics of Space*, trans. Maria Jolas (Boston: Beacon Press, 1969), pp. x and xv.

CHAPTER FOUR: *Sour Grapes*

1. In the simplicity and brevity of the implicit rural/urban contrast, "Lines" is remarkably similar to Pound's "In a Station of the Metro." The question of "influence," however, does not seem particularly relevant in this case.

2. Dated "10/18/50," the notebook contains an outline for a talk delivered in Washington, titled "Why a Writer?"

3. Untitled, uncollected poem, published in *Manuscripts*, 1 (Feb. 1922), 15.

4. Unpublished comments in the notebook described in note 2.

5. "America, Whitman, and the Art of Poetry," *The Poetry Journal*, 8 (Nov. 1917), 27–36.

6. Breslin, *William Carlos Williams, An American Artist*, p. 20.

7. "America, Whitman, and the Art of Poetry," p. 30.

8. Thomas R. Whitaker, *William Carlos Williams* (New York: Twayne, 1968), p. 56.

9. James Agee, *Let Us Now Praise Famous Men* (Boston, Houghton Mifflin, 1960), p. 469.

10. "America, Whitman, and the Art of Poetry," p. 34.

11. In this phrase, Williams may have been emulating the Cubists in their efforts to break objects down into basic geometrical forms. If so, his theory is better than his practice.

12. Unpublished in this form. It is conceivable that the phraseology, "the figure 5 / gold on red," was influenced by the prose-poem *"Anders,"* by Kandinsky, first published in 1912, which begins, *"Es war eine grosse 3—weiss auf dunkelbraun."* *Concerning the Spiritual in Art.* ed. Robert Motherwell (New York: Wittenborn, Schultz, 1947), p. 82.

13. It is a beautiful irony that Williams saw a similar fault in Charles Demuth's painting of the Williams poem, and he wrote to his painter friend to offer some quite specific suggestions for improving the picture. He sums up his dissatisfaction this way: "I feel in this picture that the completion that was once felt and made the composition a whole has been lost and that you have tried twenty times to recapture and that every try has left a trace somewhere so that the whole is tortured. It needs some new sweep of imagination through the whole to make it one" (*SL*, 97).

14. Whitaker, *William Carlos Williams*, p. 53.

15. *English Pastoral Poetry from the Beginnings to Marvell*, ed. Frank Kermode (London: George G. Harrap, 1952), p. 11.

16. *Ibid.*, pp. 12–13.

17. See also the various "pastorals" and "idyls" in Appendix A.

18. *The Poetical Works of Wordsworth*, ed. Thomas Hutchinson (London: Oxford University Press, 1960), p. 156.

19. Kermode, *English Pastoral Poetry*, p. 44.

20. See also Cary Nelson's article, "Suffused-Encircling Shapes of Mind: Inhabited Space in Williams," *Journal of Modern Literature*, 1 (May 1971), 549–564.

21. *Others For 1919, An Anthology of the New Verse*, ed. Alfred Kreymborg (New York: Nicholas L. Brown, 1920), p. 189.

CHAPTER FIVE: *Spring and All*

1. "Cooperation," *The Little Review Anthology*, ed. Margaret Anderson (New York: Hermitage House, 1953), p. 188.

2. "Our poets especially are asleep from the neck down," wrote Williams shortly before his death, giving the cliché a significant twist. "The American Idiom," *Fresco*, 1, no. 1 (1960): 16.

3. "Three Professional Studies," *The Little Review Anthology*, p. 241.

4. Whitaker, *William Carlos Williams*, p. 64.

5. Daniel-Henry Kahnweiler, *Juan Gris: His Life and Work* (New York: Abrams, 1969), p. 202.

6. *Ibid.*, pp. 200–201.

7. Quoted *ibid.*, p. 183.

8. *Ibid.*

9. Kahnweiler (*ibid.*, pp. 174ff.) is quite daring, and perhaps even correct, in his comparison of painters, poets, and composers who he believes shared the same inner dichotomies and breathed the same aesthetic ambience.

10. "Belly Music," *Others*, 5 (July 1919), 26.

11. Richard Brautigan, *The Pill Versus the Springhill Mine Disaster* (San Francisco: Delacorte, 1968), p. 43.

12. Breslin, *William Carlos Williams*, p. 75.

13. A. R. Ammons, *Collected Poems, 1951–1971* (New York: Norton, 1972), p. 147.

14. Breslin, *William Carlos Williams*, p. 75.

15. Kandinsky, *Concerning the Spiritual in Art*, p. 77.

Afterword: A Prologue

1. Ron Loewinsohn, ed., New York: New Directions, 1974.

2. A 1928 letter to Florence expresses a recurrent sentiment: "But I am an insane person—the longer I live the more I realize it—and the more I realize I am not much different from anyone else. We are all crazy—but I seem to be more so than some. Perhaps it is my only value. I simply crash all together" (*SL*, 98).

3. Hyatt H. Waggoner, *American Poets from the Puritans to the Present*, Boston: Houghton Mifflin, 1968.

4. Randall Jarrell, *Poetry and the Age* (New York: Knopf, 1953), pp. 223–224.

5. Hugh Kenner, *The Pound Era*, Berkeley: University of California Press, 1971.

6. Interview with Williams published in the New York *Herald Tribune*, January 18, 1932.

7. Not all critics agree with this judgment. Thomas R. Whitaker, while acknowledging imperfections in the composition, sees a general structural unity: "The entire sequence may be seen as enacting a

descent from auto-erotic and barren isolation (9/27, 9/29) through expansive and fructifying movements toward a new discovery of community, the past, love, and the writer's vocation . . ." (69). I just don't see it.

Index

The Early Poetry of
William Carlos Williams

Designed by R. E. Rosenbaum.
Composed by York Composition Company, Inc.,
in 11 point linotype Janson, 3 points leaded,
with display lines in monotype Deepdene.
Printed letterpress from type by York Composition Company
on Warren's No. 66 text, 50 pound basis,
with the Cornell University Press watermark.
Bound by Vail-Ballou Press, Inc.